FILLING THE EMPTY NEST

SIMPLE STRATEGIES TO REDISCOVER YOUR PURPOSE, REINVENT YOURSELF, AND REIMAGINE YOUR KIDS AS ADULTS

RICK BAPTIST

CONTENTS

INTRODUCTION

So there I was, standing in my son's bedroom, staring at his old baseball trophies. Seeing them brought a rush of memories—games played, runs scored, and afternoons spent cheering from the stands and coaching from the dugout. My heart was full reflecting on the joy and pride of those times. Fifteen years of fun, emotions, and bonding all packed into one little space. Now, they just felt like relics from the Jurassic age.

The house was quiet. Too quiet. I could hear the clock ticking, and I swear I heard the dust settle. And to think, I had two more rooms just like this! My kids had flown the nest, and I was left wondering what to do with all these trophies and, well, the rest of my life. Welcome to the empty nest, folks—a place where you might find yourself sobbing into your morning coffee one minute and then planning a spontaneous weekend getaway the next.

This book is about navigating that crazy, wonderful, and often messy space called the empty nest. It's about finding a new purpose, reinventing yourself, and figuring out how to relate to your kids now that they're adults. You heard me right - your kids are adults now! It's about tackling this new chapter with grace (and a good sense of humor). We'll talk about real strategies for rediscovering who you are beyond the role of parent. We'll also dive into how to keep those family ties strong, even as they stretch across cities or time zones.

I wrote this book for you because I get it! We're Generation X parents (or maybe young Millennials), raised on landlines and mixtapes, using FaceTime to keep up with our always-busy kids. You're balancing modern parenting with a world that seems to change every five minutes. You've faced challenges that your parents never even imagined, and now you're staring down another one—the empty nest.

Let's be honest. This transition is an emotional rollercoaster. One moment, you're thrilled with the freedom to binge-watch your favorite shows without interruption. The next, you find yourself missing the chaos of a full house. It's completely normal to feel a mix of loss, loneliness, and excitement. I've been there. I've felt the echoes of an empty home and the thrill of new opportunities. I've wrestled with letting go and embracing what comes next. The good news? Totally normal behavior.

Allow me to share a bit more about my journey. I'm Rick, a proud parent of three incredible kids, each with their own unique path. My life has been a tapestry of roles: from the nurturing stay-at-home dad juggling household chores and playdates, the dedicated baseball coach shouting encouragement, and the committed professional managing the demands of a 40-hour workweek. Navigating the transition of letting my children go was a profound challenge, filled with moments of pride, uncertainty, and reflection. Throughout my journey, my children have been unwitting teachers, imparting lessons of patience, resilience, and the profound impact of unconditional love. These emotionally charged experiences have shaped the insights and strategies I share in this book, enriching it with a depth that mirrors our collective journey through parenthood.

This book is laid out to guide you through this new chapter. We'll tackle subjects like single parenting, changes in family dynamics, and the looming role of being a spoiling grandparent. Each chapter builds on the last, weaving a comprehensive guide designed to help you find your footing. There's a lot here to explore! Take from this book as much as you wish. You'll find some helpful advice on parenting your parent - maybe that's not you, but I bet you know a friend who's needing some answers. Share these stories with them.

But here's the thing: this isn't just a book full of theories. It's packed with practical tips and strategies you can put into action. There are exercises and checklists to help you engage with the material. You'll find actionable advice that fits into real life, not just a textbook. What sets this book apart is its focus on the unique perspectives of our generation. With a mix of humor and personal stories, we're stepping away from old-fashioned views and bringing a fresh, relatable voice to the conversation. I'm speaking directly to you about all your unique experiences and challenges.

I invite you to look at the empty nest not as an end but as a beginning. It's a chance for personal growth and reinvention. This is your opportunity to pursue dreams you've put on hold, explore new interests, and redefine your relationships with your kids—eventually, at least! We will get there together.

As we wrap up this introduction, let me leave you with this: you're not alone. This book will be your companion on this journey, offering support, laughter, and a little bit of wisdom. You can thrive in this new phase of life, I promise! Let's get started.

1

SO ... THAT JUST HAPPENED

You know that moment when you're sitting in your living room, and suddenly, it feels like you've walked into someone else's house? That's how it feels when the kids move out. The once vibrant, noisy home filled with laughter, arguments over Wi-Fi, and the eternal mystery of missing socks is now eerily quiet. You find yourself staring at the empty spaces and wondering when your house turned into a museum. It's true! It's like that moment when you're watching a movie and the screen goes black, leaving you with just the credits—except this isn't a film; it's your life. And no one handed you a script for this scene. But as the quiet settles in, so does something else: the strange new freedom to do whatever you want. With that comes a mix of emotions that can feel like a rollercoaster you didn't sign up for. On the one hand, there's the sadness of seeing the kids grow up and fly the coop. There's absolutely depression to fight. But on the other, there's the tantalizing freedom to rediscover who you are outside of being a parent.

1.1 THE EMOTIONAL ROLLERCOASTER: NAVIGATING FEELINGS OF LOSS AND FREEDOM

The reality of the empty nest is that it's a cocktail of emotions, shaken, not stirred. You're proud of your kids; they've grown into fantastic adults. But there's the catch: they're adults. No more impromptu late-night chats or family game nights where someone inevitably flips the Monopoly board. It's all part of the duality of this transition. One minute, you're basking in the pride of their achievements, and the next, you're longing for the days when you had to referee a sibling spat. It's like feeling both the warmth of a summer day and the chill of an unexpected breeze simultaneously. One parent I spoke with, let's call her Jane, put it perfectly. She said, "I'm so proud of my son for getting that job in another city, but I'd give anything to trip over his shoes in the hallway one more time." Jane's experience is shared, and I love that analogy. Many parents find themselves caught between pride and a profound sense of loneliness, triggered by small things like walking past a room that used to be filled with life or stumbling upon a forgotten toy in the attic.

When her youngest daughter left for college, Mary thought she was prepared. She had read all the articles, talked to friends, and told herself this was the natural order of things. But as she walked back into her now-quiet home, the emptiness hit her like a wave. The once-bustling house was eerily silent, and she found herself wandering from room to room, unsure of what to do with the sudden stillness. For weeks, Mary tried to fill the void with busy work—cleaning, organizing and even taking up a few new hobbies. But none of it could shake the hollow feeling. The house didn't just feel empty; she felt empty. She missed the noise, the chaos, the constant presence of her kids. One afternoon, she sat at the kitchen table, looking at a stack of old family photos, and let the tears come.

It's absolutely a huge mountain to climb. But there's good news, too. You can manage these feelings and even turn them into something positive. The first step is to allow yourself to feel what you're feeling. Don't bottle up the sadness and pretend it's not there. Acknowledge it. One effective way to process these emotions is through journaling. Writing down your thoughts can be incredibly cathartic, like having a conversation with yourself without the awkward silence. Start with something simple: jot down how you feel each day, even if it's just a word or two. This simple practice can help you track your emotional journey and identify patterns over time. Breathing exercises can also be a great ally. When you feel anxiety creeping in, take a few deep breaths, hold them, and let them out slowly. It's incredible how a little oxygen can clear your head. And remember, you're not alone in this. Reach out to friends or join a support group to share experiences and advice. Sometimes, just knowing that others are riding the same rollercoaster can be comforting.

While it may feel like you're losing something, there's also a tremendous opportunity for growth. Think of this phase as a chance to transform, much like a caterpillar turning into a butterfly. With the kids out of the house, you have the time to explore interests you may have set aside. The possibilities are endless, whether that's starting a new hobby like painting or taking up a sport you've always wanted to try. I've met parents who've taken this time to travel, learn new languages, or even start businesses. They've found joy and fulfillment in pursuits they never had time for. So, while the empty nest may begin with a feeling of loss, it's also a blank canvas waiting for you to paint your next chapter.

1.2 TRANSFORMING SADNESS: FINDING JOY IN THE QUIET MOMENTS

Picture this: you wake up not to the sound of a blaring alarm but to the gentle hum of morning light filtering through your window. The house is still. There's no one to drive to school or practice. It's just you, your thoughts, and the world waking up outside. Solitude, once feared, can become a sanctuary if you let it. Embracing these quiet moments can lead to a profound sense of peace and self-discovery. Think of it as a gift wrapped in silence. This is the perfect time to explore a morning routine that sets a positive tone for your day. Start with a few minutes of mindfulness. Sit with your cup of coffee or tea, savoring the aroma and warmth. Let each sip ground you in the present moment. This simple act can become a cherished ritual, a time just for you to reflect and set intentions for the day ahead.

Creating a personal sanctuary in your home can also provide comfort. Whether it's a cozy reading nook, a meditation corner, or a garden spot, find a space that speaks to you. Fill it with items that bring you joy—books, plants, soft lighting. This is your retreat, where you can escape the world's chaos and find solace. It doesn't have to be grand, just somewhere you feel completely at ease. And it doesn't have to be one of your kid's rooms! Not yet, anyway.

With the newfound quiet, you can cultivate new rituals and habits. Perhaps a weekly solo activity becomes your new norm. Imagine taking a walk in nature every Saturday morning, where you can lose yourself in the beauty around you and find clarity in your thoughts. Nature has a way of calming the mind and sparking creativity. Maybe you could also pick up a creative hobby like painting, knitting, or even woodworking? These activities not only fill your time but also bring a sense of accomplishment and joy.

Quiet moments are ripe for creativity and productivity. Reframe them as opportunities rather than voids to be filled. You might find yourself inspired to start a small home project or take up gardening. There's something incredibly satisfying about planting a seed and watching it grow, a metaphor for your own growth in this phase of life. For those who enjoy writing, consider setting aside time each week for self-exploration through writing. Use prompts that challenge you to think deeply about your desires, fears, and dreams. This exercise can lead to insights and a deeper understanding of yourself.

Give it a shot! There's no need for hesitation—after all, this is your time without interruptions or distractions.

Interactive Element: Writing Prompts for Self-Exploration

1. What is one thing you've always wanted to learn, and why?
2. Describe a moment in your life when you felt truly at peace.
3. What are three things you're grateful for today, and how do they impact your life?

4. Write about a place that brings you joy. What makes it unique?
5. Reflect on a challenge you've overcome and the strengths you discovered in yourself.

As you navigate this new chapter, remember to celebrate small wins. Keep a gratitude journal to document these victories, no matter how minor they seem. Celebrating doesn't have to be elaborate—a simple toast with your favorite beverage or a quiet moment of reflection can be enough. Recognizing these achievements reinforces positivity and helps you see your progress.

Organize mini celebrations for personal milestones. You could have finally finished that novel you've been reading or completed a home project. These are moments worth acknowledging. Invite a friend for coffee, or take yourself out for a treat. It's about recognizing that life goes on even in the quiet moments, and there is joy to be found.

Transforming sadness into joy doesn't happen overnight, but with intentional effort, the quiet moments that once seemed daunting can become some of the most fulfilling. Embrace solitude, cultivate new rituals, and celebrate your accomplishments. This is your time to rediscover joy, and in doing so, you'll find that the empty nest isn't so empty after all.

1.3 THE ART OF LETTING GO: TRUSTING YOUR CHILD'S INDEPENDENCE

Letting go is a phrase that sounds deceptively simple until you're the one holding on for dear life. As parents, we spend years teaching our kids how to walk, talk, and think, and then suddenly, we're supposed to just step back and watch them use all those skills to leave us behind. It's like spending years building a magnificent sandcastle only to watch the tide sweep it away. But, just as the tide brings change, it also brings growth. Allowing our children to forge their paths is crucial for their development and our peace of mind. It's a paradox, really. By letting them go, we give them the space to become who they're meant to be. This independence is not just a rite of passage for them; it's an opportunity to witness the fantastic adults they've become. Psychologically, this autonomy is vital for young adults. It gives them the confidence to make decisions, face challenges, and learn from their mistakes. It's like giving them the keys to their life and watching them drive off into the sunset —hopefully at a safe speed. I've seen many parents go through this transition, and while it's never easy, the rewards are immense. There was this one couple I knew who, after their son moved to another city for work, found themselves in a bittersweet state of pride and emptiness. They described it as watching a bird finally take flight after years of nesting. Their son flourished, building a life filled with new friendships and experiences while maintaining a close, albeit different, relationship with his parents.

Letting go doesn't mean you disappear from your child's life. It means stepping back just enough to let them step forward. A technique that has proven beneficial for numerous parents is meditation centered around the theme of release. This practice involves finding a quiet moment to sit, gently acknowledging your thoughts and emotions without critique, and then consciously letting them go. It serves as an emotional reset, a kind of mental purification, stripping away the clutter of 'what ifs' and 'maybes' that can overwhelm our thoughts. It's like hitting the reset button on your emotional state. Picture it as a mental decluttering session, clearing out the 'what ifs' and 'maybes' that tend to clutter our minds. Another approach is writing a letter of encouragement to your child. This is not just a way to express your hopes and dreams for them; it's also an opportunity to let go of your worries. Tell them about your pride in their achievements, your confidence in their abilities, and your excitement for their future. Then, seal the letter and give it to them, or keep it as a reminder to yourself of the trust you have in their journey.

You remain vital to their support system even as you step back. The trick here is to offer support without inadvertently reverting to your previous role as the all-knowing parent. This is where setting up regular check-ins can be beneficial. Agree on times that work for both parties, respecting each other's schedules. It could be a weekly call or a monthly dinner. These check-ins are not just about keeping tabs; they're a chance to connect, share updates, and offer support when needed. Establishing mutual expectations for communication can also help. Discuss how often you'd like to hear from each other and what forms of communication work best. They may be more comfortable texting than talking or prefer a quick video call. The key is to find a balance that respects their autonomy while keeping the lines of communication open.

Of course, life has a way of throwing curveballs, and there may be times when your child stumbles. They might face setbacks or even return home for a while. It's crucial to handle these situations with grace and understanding. Have a contingency plan for when the nest unexpectedly fills up again. This could involve setting some ground rules for living arrangements or discussing timelines for their stay (we will visit this later). Encourage them to approach these setbacks as learning opportunities. Help them develop resilience and problem-solving skills by offering guidance when asked but resisting the urge to solve all their problems. Remember, the goal is to support them in finding solutions, not to hand them a ready-made answer. As they navigate these challenges, remind them—and yourself—

that setbacks are not failures. They are simply steps along the path to independence.

1.4 FROM CAREGIVER TO CONSULTANT: REDEFINING YOUR ROLE

In your non-so-distant past, you were most likely the leading figure in your household's daily operations, and everyone knew it -- how often did you hear, "What's for lunch today, mom?" Today, you find yourself stepping into a role that feels more akin to a corporate advisor - a consultant. Sound familiar? That's exactly what this phase is about: shifting from the hands-on, day-to-day caregiving role to one where you're more of a supportive guide. This doesn't mean you're stepping into any kind of irrelevance but into a new kind of relevance. As a caregiver, you were the immediate go-to for every crisis, big or small. Now, as a consultant, your advice is still valuable but offered with a touch more reservation and a lot more listening. You're there to provide insights when asked, to help navigate life's ups and downs, but without the overbearing presence that parenting young children sometimes requires. I mean, we are really going to miss those tantrums in the supermarket, am I right?

This new role involves a different style of communication. Consider it a shift from giving orders to offering suggestions. Imagine sitting in a cozy café, sipping coffee with your child, who now occasionally calls you by your first name instead of "Mom" or "Dad" when they feel particularly independent. Oh boy! Regardless of your new name, It's about giving advice that feels collaborative. Instead of saying, "You should do this," try, "Have you thought about this approach?" It's a subtle difference, but it makes your child feel respected in their decision-making process. Active listening is essential here. It means genuinely hearing what they're saying without immediately jumping in with solutions. Sometimes, they need a sounding board more than they need a fix. This listening approach builds trust and strengthens your relationship, showing you value their perspective.

Communicating effectively with adult children requires a delicate balance. You want to offer guidance without infringing on their autonomy. Techniques like using "I" statements can be helpful. For example, instead of saying, "You never call anymore," try, "I miss our chats." This shift makes the conversation feel less like an accusation and more like an expression of your feelings. Constructive feedback should focus on the issue, not past grievances. It's about addressing current matters with a forward-looking perspective rather than dwelling on what went wrong before. The goal is to foster a dialogue that's open and honest, where both parties feel heard and respected.

Setting boundaries might sound daunting, but it's crucial for a healthy relationship. Think of it as putting up fences with gates. They're not there to keep anyone out but to define spaces clearly. Creating a family agreement on independence can be a helpful exercise. Sit down together and discuss what autonomy looks like for both of you. It could be about agreeing on how often to check in or setting rules for when they visit home. These conversations lay the groundwork for mutual respect and understanding. One example of a boundary-setting conversation might be this: you say, "I'd love for us to have dinner together once a month. How does that sound to you?" This approach shows you're interested in maintaining connection while respecting their schedule and independence.

As you settle into this new role, embrace it with pride. You're not losing your place in their lives; you're redefining it. Many parents have found immense satisfaction in this transition.

They've discovered that stepping back a little allows their children to confidently step forward. It's like watching a garden you've tended for years bloom in new and unexpected ways. One parent shared how she reframed her role from manager to mentor. She found joy in being the person her child called for advice rather than instructions! Her child's growth and independence became a source of pride rather than a loss.

The role of a parent changes, but the value you bring to your child's life doesn't diminish. In fact, it takes on a new depth. By embracing this new role as a mentor and advisor, you continue to be an integral part of their lives. It's about offering wisdom gleaned from years of experience without dictating the path they should take. This shift strengthens your relationship and helps you grow as an individual. You're learning, adapting, and thriving alongside your children, proving that life, like parenting, is ever-evolving and full of potential. And yes, you can do this. But first, it's time to tackle an essential part of the journey.

2

WAIT, WHO EVEN AM I NOW?

There comes a moment when you glance in the mirror and do a double-take. Not because you've suddenly sprouted a new wrinkle or gray hair but because you're staring at a reflection that seems a stranger. It's as if you've been cast in a new role, but no one handed you the script. I will never forget the first time I called out my daughter's name, expecting to hear the usual sweet or sassy response, and ... nothing. The kids have moved out, and with them, the familiar routines that have defined you for so long. The house is quieter, and you—well, you're left wondering who you are now that "Mom" or "Dad" isn't the top line on your résumé.

When the children leave, many parents experience what I like to call the "void vortex." It's that unsettling feeling of emptiness, a lack of direction that spins you into a reflective abyss. You're not alone in this! I've spoken with numerous parents who faced this identity crisis head-on. Take Lisa, for instance. She spent years driving carpools and coordinating soccer snacks, and when her youngest left for college, she found herself questioning what she'd do with all her free time. "Is it too late to become an astronaut?" she jokingly pondered, only half-seriously. Psychologists say this is a common phenomenon, where identity loss can lead to feelings of sadness and confusion. It's a normal part of the transition, a moment to hit pause and reassess who you are beneath the layers of parenthood.

Recognizing your individual worth beyond the title of parent is paramount. You've poured love and energy into raising your children for years, but now it's time to turn some of that nurturing spirit inward. Boosting self-esteem can start with simple exercises. Reflect on your achievements, big and small. Did you once play an instrument, lead a project at work, or even whip up a legendary lasagna? These are parts of you that hold value. Create a list of these accomplishments and revisit it regularly. Remember that your worth isn't solely tied to your children's successes. You are a person of incredible substance, with talents and passions that deserve recognition.

Self-reflection exercises can help you explore your identity beyond parenting roles. Start with a mirror exercise. Stand in front of your reflection and speak positive affirmations aloud. It might feel awkward at first, but words have power. Tell yourself, "I am strong, I am capable, I am enough." Believe it because it's true. Let's open up that new journal, shall we? Consider prompts like, "What brings me joy?" or "What dreams have I set aside?" Let your thoughts flow freely without judgment. Writing can illuminate aspects of yourself that have been overshadowed by the demands of parenting.

Interactive Element: Self-Reflection Journaling Prompts

1. Describe a time when you felt truly fulfilled. What were you doing?
2. What are three things you love about yourself that have nothing to do with being a parent?
3. If you could try anything new without fear, what would it be?
4. What is one value that has guided you throughout your life?
5. Write a letter to your future self detailing hopes and dreams for the next chapter.

Building a new self-image is not about discarding the past but expanding upon it. Consider crafting a vision statement for your life. What values and goals do you want to pursue? This statement acts as a compass, guiding you toward a future that aligns with your desires. Visualization techniques are empowering. Picture yourself achieving a personal goal, whether it's running a marathon, writing a book, or learning a new skill. Find that old passion and focus on it like you used to. Close your eyes and see it in vivid detail—feel the emotions, hear the sounds, taste the victory. No seriously, do it! I'll wait here.

Okay, ready? Here we go.

2.1 PASSION PROJECTS: UNEARTHING FORGOTTEN DREAMS

Remember those hobbies you used to love before life got in the way? Maybe it was photography, writing, or playing the guitar. If you're like many parents, you've probably shelved a few passions over the years. Now's the time to dust them off and see if they still spark joy. It's like opening an old, forgotten box in the attic—who knows what treasures you might find? Start by asking yourself some reflective questions: What activities made you lose track of time? What did you dream of becoming when you were younger? Sometimes, flipping through past notebooks or diaries can reignite that flicker of excitement. You might stumble upon sketches of a dream project or lists of places you want to visit. If you're feeling crafty, create a vision board. Fill it with images and words that resonate with your aspirations. This isn't just about nostalgia; it's about visualizing a future that excites you.

Once you've rediscovered those forgotten dreams, it's time to make them a reality. Take the story of Mike, a father who always wanted to open a café. With his kids off to college, he finally pursued that dream. He started small, hosting pop-up events before leasing a permanent space. It helped him fill the void! And you don't need piles of cash to make a dream come true, either. Vanessa, always interested in doodling and art but never finding the time or energy to examine the digital art world, finally dropped a couple hundred bucks on a drawing tablet. Little steps leading to a fulfilling artist-for-hire? Why not? These success stories remind us that starting something new is never too late. First, outline the steps needed to bring your project to life. Research your market and draft a simple business plan if it's a business. For creative pursuits, set specific goals. Want to write a novel? Start with a chapter outline and a writing schedule. Break down more giant dreams into manageable tasks. Commit to a timeline, but leave room for flexibility. The key is to take action, however small, and build momentum.

Balancing passion projects with everyday responsibilities can feel like juggling flaming swords—they're exciting but risky if not handled carefully. This is where time management becomes your best ally. Consider using planners or apps to schedule dedicated time slots for your passions. Treat these appointments as seriously as you would a business meeting. Prioritization is crucial. Identify your top three daily tasks and allocate the necessary time. It's okay to say no to some commitments to make room for what truly matters. Remember, this isn't about perfect balance; it's about integration. Your passions should complement your life, not overwhelm it.

Finding community support can breathe life into your passion projects. Seek out groups or forums with like-minded individuals who share your interests. Online platforms are great for connecting people worldwide, but pay attention to local meetups or clubs. These communities offer encouragement, advice, and sometimes just a sympathetic ear when things get tough. Whether it's a photography group that meets for weekend shoots or a writers' workshop critiquing each other's work, these networks provide invaluable motivation. They also hold you accountable, ensuring you stay on track with your goals. Plus, sharing your journey with others can make the process more enjoyable. After all, pursuing your passions isn't just about personal fulfillment; it's also about building connections and creating memories along the way.

2.2 HOBBIES AND JOY: MISSION POSSIBLE

Okay, it's Saturday morning, sunlight is streaming through the windows, and you're not racing off to a soccer game or chauffeuring teenagers around town. Instead, you're sipping coffee, pondering what truly brings you joy. It's like being handed a blank canvas and all the colors in the world to paint with. The challenge? Figuring out which colors to use. Identifying hobbies might initially feel daunting, but it's also a delightful adventure. Think back to activities that have always intrigued you. It could be photography, pottery, or even beekeeping. Yes, beekeeping—that could be your thing! There are countless hobbies, from the familiar to the downright quirky. If you're stuck, try taking a hobby quiz online. These can offer surprising insights and point you toward interests you never considered. Lists of potential hobbies can provide a starting point, and a bit of trial and error can turn the mundane into the extraordinary.

Once you've identified a hobby, the next step is weaving it into your daily life, like adding a new stitch to your favorite sweater. It's all about creating a rhythm that feels natural. Start by carving out time in your calendar. It doesn't have to be hours; even 15 minutes daily can work wonders. Treat this time as sacred, a non-negotiable appointment with yourself. You might be surprised how quickly those minutes add up to something substantial. Think of hobbies as mini-vacations from routine, offering a respite and a chance to rejuvenate. Integrating them into your daily schedule means you're not just filling time; you're enriching it. The joy of hobbies is in their simplicity—they're pursuits you engage in for the love of it, without the pressure of perfection or productivity.

The benefits of hobbies stretch far beyond just filling time. They positively impact mental and physical health, acting as a balm for the soul. Studies have shown that engaging in hobbies can reduce stress, boost mood, and even improve cognitive function. Think of hobbies as a workout for your brain, keeping it agile and engaged. Parents who've embraced hobbies often report feeling more balanced and energized. Take Sarah, a mom who took up painting after her kids moved out. She discovered that mixing colors on a canvas was therapeutic and a way to express herself in ways words couldn't. After years of focusing on her kids, Jane discovered a love for gardening when the house became quieter. What started as a small weekend project quickly grew into her favorite way to unwind and reconnect with herself. Testimonials like these highlight the transformative power of hobbies. They're not just pastimes; they're lifelines to well-being.

Sharing your hobby can transform a solitary activity into a communal experience. Invite friends or family over for a casual evening where everyone brings a project they're working on. Think of it as a modern-day quilting bee, where creativity flows alongside conversation. Teaching someone your newfound skill can also be rewarding. Whether it's showing a friend how to knit or organizing a photography outing, sharing hobbies builds connections and creates shared memories. These gatherings become more than just social events; they're opportunities to deepen relationships and inspire others to explore their interests. Through hobbies, you find joy in the doing and sharing, turning personal fulfillment into a shared journey.

A lot of us have created and enjoyed hobbies with our children when they were at home. Don't be selfish - share! Growing up, my mother and I developed habits and hobbies we enjoyed together - baseball games, puzzles, and board games ... she even took me to a couple of pro wrestling matches! Now, I don't think she bought any tickets to secretly see Hulk Hogan when I went to college. Maybe she did! But we've kept up these shared interests all my life; we share all those old memories and make new ones. We even occasionally watch Wrestlemania together! My mom is pretty cool, right? All right, it's time to get to work.

2.3 CAREER SHIFTS: EXPLORING NEW PROFESSIONAL HORIZONS

As you clock in for another shift in the morning, a thought bubbles up—is this really what you want to do for the rest of your life? For many, the empty nest is a wake-up call, a reminder that it's okay to evaluate where you stand in your career. Start by taking a good, hard look at your current job satisfaction. Are you excited to tackle each day, or do you find yourself hitting snooze a few too many times? Maybe you've been holding on to your job because alternatives mean less money. Perhaps the financial burden has meant taking on a second job in recent years, stretching your capacity to its limits. It's a testament to human resilience how we can manage and endure less-than-ideal situations to secure our family's needs and future.

Once you've gotten a clearer picture, it's time to explore opportunities that align with your passions and skills. This isn't about throwing caution to the wind and quitting your day job on a whim. It's about being strategic and thoughtful. Networking becomes your secret weapon, allowing you to connect with individuals who might open doors to new possibilities. Attend industry events, join professional groups, and don't underestimate the power of LinkedIn. Online courses and workshops offer a chance to upskill or even pivot entirely. Whether it's a coding boot camp or a creative writing course, these platforms are treasure troves of knowledge waiting to be tapped into.

So, you've done the groundwork, and now it's time for the leap—a career transition. Crafting a compelling resume is your first step. Highlight transferable skills and experiences that relate to your new path. Think of it as your professional story, with each line a chapter leading up to this moment. There are countless stories of successful mid-life career transitions, reminding us it's never too late to follow your calling. Take the example of a former accountant who became a yoga instructor. She found fulfillment in helping others find balance, both literally and figuratively. These narratives inspire and reassure that a change in direction can be gratifying.

Pursuing a new career might be thrilling, but let's not forget the practical side—maintaining financial stability. Planning is key. Assess your financial situation and create a roadmap that accommodates this shift. Consider starting with a side hustle, testing the waters before diving headfirst. It's like dipping your toes into the pool before a swim. A side hustle can provide financial support while allowing you to explore your passion. Whether it's freelance writing, consulting, or selling handmade goods, these ventures can serve as stepping stones toward a full-fledged career change. Balancing a new career pursuit with existing responsibilities might seem daunting. Still, it's entirely possible with careful planning and a bit of courage. Embrace this phase with enthusiasm and a sense of adventure.

After all, I'm writing this book, am I not? Could I be filing my void vortex? You bet!

2.4 SIDE HUSTLES AND NEW VENTURES: EXPLORING OPPORTUNITIES

The empty nest may leave a gap in your daily routine. Still, it also opens up opportunities to explore new income streams. Imagine the freedom to transform your passions and skills into something profitable. It's like having a blank canvas and a palette full of possibilities. Freelance work is a fantastic start. Whether you're a whiz with words, numbers, or design, there's a market hungry for your expertise. Consider consulting in your field or tapping into the gig economy, where your skills can shine on a flexible schedule. And if you've got a knack for entrepreneurship, why not start a small business or an online store? Selling handmade crafts, curated vintage finds, or even your homemade jam can turn a hobby into a thriving venture. The internet has made it easier than ever to reach a global audience, so don't be afraid to dream big.

Leverage those existing skills you've honed over the years—skills that might have been sidelined while you focused on raising a family. If you're a former teacher, tutoring or hosting workshops could be your ticket. Do you have a flair for photography or crafting? Turn that into a profitable hobby. People love unique, handmade items, and there's always demand for personal, heartfelt creations. It's about recognizing that what you consider a simple pastime could be someone else's treasure. By monetizing these skills, you generate income and share your talent with the world. And who knows? You might discover a new passion in the process.

Before diving headfirst into a new venture, it's wise to research market demand. This means understanding what people want, what they're willing to pay for, and what gaps exist in the market. Conducting surveys or focus groups can provide invaluable insights. Analyze your competitors to see what they're doing well—and where they might be missing the mark. This isn't about copying; it's about finding your unique angle. Social media platforms are gold mines for promotion. Use them to share your journey, gather feedback, and connect with potential customers. Entrepreneurial networks or forums can offer support, advice, and collaboration opportunities. These communities are filled with people who've been where you are, ready to share their wisdom and experiences.

Developing a business plan is like drawing a map for your entrepreneurial journey. It doesn't have to be complicated, but it should outline your goals, objectives, and the steps needed to get there. Start with what you want to achieve and why. Then, work out the logistics—what resources you'll need, how you'll market your product or service, and how you'll manage your finances. Financial projections and budgeting are crucial. They ensure you understand the costs and what you need to break even or profit. This plan is your roadmap, guiding you through the challenges and triumphs of starting something new. It gives you direction but leaves room for adaptation and growth as you learn and evolve.

2.5 THE BUCKET LIST: SETTING NEW PERSONAL GOALS

Let's face it, when the kids were home, the idea of a bucket list might have seemed like a distant dream, buried under laundry piles and PTA meetings. But now, the empty nest phase offers a golden opportunity to dust off those old ambitions and make them a reality. Creating a meaningful bucket list isn't about skydiving or climbing Everest—unless that's your thing. It's about identifying what excites you, whether big or small. To start, consider using a bucket list template. These can help frame your thoughts, turning vague aspirations into concrete, actionable items. Think about what you want to achieve in the next year, five years, or even a decade. Use goal-setting techniques that break these dreams into achievable milestones, like learning a new language or traveling to a new country yearly.

Once you have your list, the next step is prioritizing these goals to ensure they're realistic. You don't want to avoid setting yourself up for failure by trying to do everything at once. Instead, focus on time-bound goals, using the SMART criteria: Specific,

Measurable, Achievable, Relevant, and Time-bound. This method helps in setting clear objectives and timelines. Visualization exercises can also be beneficial. Picture yourself achieving each goal, feeling the emotions, and celebrating the triumphs. This mental imagery can motivate you, keeping you focused and driven.

Of course, no bucket list is complete without its share of obstacles. Life has a way of throwing curveballs, but that shouldn't derail your dreams. Developing problem-solving skills is crucial. Consider using worksheets that identify potential hurdles and brainstorm solutions. Sometimes, an inspirational quote or story can reignite your passion when things get tough. Remember, persistence is critical. You're bound to encounter setbacks, but each challenge is an opportunity to learn and grow.

As you tick off each item on your bucket list, make sure to celebrate your achievements. It doesn't matter if it's a small victory or a significant milestone—each deserves recognition. Plan celebratory events to mark these occasions, whether it's a dinner with friends or a solo retreat. Create a memory book of accomplishments filled with photos, mementos, and reflections on what each goal meant to you. This book will serve as a testament to your dedication and inspire you to keep dreaming.

In the grand scheme, your bucket list is more than just a collection of goals. It reflects who you are and who you aspire to be. As the nest empties, it fills with the possibility of new beginnings. Embrace this chapter with enthusiasm and curiosity, knowing that the best is yet to come. Now, with these personal goals in your pocket, let's explore the broader scope of relationships and connections in the next chapter.

3

FIND YOUR CREW, BUILD YOUR TRIBE

So, you've got the quiet house, the extra time, and maybe even a newfound hobby or two. But let's be honest—this journey can feel a little lonely sometimes, can't it? As much as we might enjoy our solo time, humans are wired for connection. That's why building a new community at this stage in life isn't just a bonus; it's essential. The friends who get you, who celebrate the little things with you, and who know exactly what it means to watch your kids fly off—that's your crew, your tribe. Finding that community isn't about simply filling time; it's about adding richness and meaning to this new chapter. Ready to find your people?

Community is more than just a buzzword. It's a lifeline that keeps us grounded and connected, especially as we navigate the empty nest phase. Research from Stanford Lifestyle Medicine suggests that social connections are crucial for successful aging and overall well-being. Loneliness and social isolation, on the other hand, can pose health risks equivalent to smoking or obesity. Who knew chatting over a card game could be as important as hitting the gym? Positive social interactions release dopamine, that feel-good neurotransmitter that keeps us returning for more. So, while our nests may be empty, our social calendars shouldn't be.

To find the right community, start by identifying your interests and values. Are you a book lover, an outdoor enthusiast, or someone passionate about social justice? There's a group for everyone. Interest-based communities, like book clubs or hiking groups, offer a sense of belonging and shared purpose. If you're driven by values, consider joining organizations that align with your beliefs, such as environmental groups or community service clubs. These communities provide more than just companionship; they offer a platform to engage in activities that resonate with your passions. And the best part? You get to share these experiences with others who care just as much as you do.

Exploring local community resources is a great way to start building your tribe. Libraries and community centers are often hubs of activity, offering everything from yoga classes to art workshops. They're like the Swiss Army knives of social engagement. Don't overlook neighborhood associations, either. They can be treasure troves of local events, offering everything from block parties to volunteer opportunities. They're also fantastic for getting to know the nearby folks, turning neighbors into friends who can swap more than cookie recipes.

Building a support network takes time, but it's worth the effort. Begin by attending networking events or meetups tailored to your interests. Approach them with an open mind and a willingness to strike up conversations. It's a bit like dating but without the romantic pressure. Be genuine, ask questions, and listen actively. People appreciate authenticity, and it's the best way to forge meaningful connections. When you meet someone new, suggest a follow-up meeting, whether a shared drink or a walk in the park. These small gestures can turn acquaintances into friends.

Interactive Element: Tips for Approaching New People

1. **Be Yourself:** Authenticity is key. People are drawn to genuine personalities, so let your true self shine.
2. **Find Common Ground:** Start with a shared interest or experience. It's an easy way to break the ice and keep the conversation flowing.
3. **Ask Open-Ended Questions:** Encourage dialogue by asking questions that require more than a yes or no answer.
4. **Listen Actively:** Show interest in what the other person is saying. Nod, make eye contact, and follow up with related questions.
5. **Follow Up:** If you hit it off, suggest meeting again. It could be as simple as exchanging phone numbers or connecting via social media.

The beauty of building a community lies in its diversity. A well-rounded support network is like a patchwork quilt, each piece unique yet essential to the whole. Surround yourself with people from different walks of life, each bringing their perspectives and experiences. This diversity enriches your interactions, offering fresh insights and broadening your horizons. You'll find meaningful relationships can form in the most unexpected places, from a serendipitous meeting at a local event to a casual chat over a mutual hobby.

Of course, the digital age offers a unique opportunity to meet people from the comfort of your own home. Online communities, social media groups, and interest-based forums like Facebook groups allow you to find like-minded individuals who share your hobbies and passions. Whether it's joining a virtual book club, participating in online fitness classes, or simply engaging in casual conversations, the internet provides countless ways to forge new friendships. There are also plenty of local opportunities that use the internet to market, so if you're avoiding going online, you might be missing out.

Connecting with others is a rewarding endeavor that can enhance (or pleasantly distract you from) your empty nest experience. It offers a sense of purpose and belonging, providing support and camaraderie as you navigate this new chapter. So go ahead, embrace the challenge, and discover the joy of connecting with others. Your tribe is out there, waiting to be found.

3.1 VOLUNTEER VENTURES: GIVING BACK TO GAIN MORE

Reflecting on those hectic weekends filled with my children's sports activities—basketball at 10 am for son, softball at 11 am for daughter, and soccer for both in the afternoon—I recall frequent stops at fast-food drive-throughs. Amid those rushed moments, the occasional request to add a donation for a charitable cause would arise. While the intention to contribute was there, such fleeting transactions always felt insufficient, a mere drop in the bucket compared to meaningful engagement. Not to mention, I needed the money for the burrito. Life was a blur then, and the opportunity for deeper involvement didn't come as often.

Well, these days, you might find you have a lot more time and a couple extra dollars. Not only that, but you've also gained experience and a desire to contribute. Enter volunteering—a gateway to purpose and fulfillment waiting for you to walk through. Volunteering is more than just filling time; it's about using your talents and passions to make a tangible difference. Whether you're a whiz at organizing, have a knack for teaching, or love lending a hand, a local non-profit or charity is eager for your help. These organizations often operate on shoestring budgets and rely heavily on volunteers to keep running. They need people like you, who bring skills and a wealth of life experience.

Imagine teaching a financial literacy class to young adults or mentoring a budding entrepreneur. Skill-based volunteer opportunities are a fantastic way to share what you know while igniting a spark in someone else. You might even discover new skills along the way. Volunteering isn't just about giving; it's a two-way street that allows you to learn and grow. You could find yourself leading a team to organize a local event or using your creativity to run a community art program. It's about finding that sweet spot where your interests and the community's needs intersect, creating something beautiful and impactful.

The personal benefits of volunteering are as rewarding as the tangible impact you make. Studies have shown that volunteering increases happiness and a stronger sense of purpose. It's like a workout for your soul, releasing endorphins and boosting your mood. When you volunteer, you connect with others, which can help alleviate feelings of loneliness and isolation. It gives you a reason to get up in the morning, a sense of belonging, and the satisfaction of contributing to something bigger than yourself. Volunteering can also introduce you to new friends who share your interests and values, expanding your social circle meaningfully.

Making a difference in your community can be as simple as organizing a local food drive or participating in a long-term volunteer commitment. These activities are fulfilling and build stronger, more resilient communities. You could help plant a community garden, tutor kids after school, or assist at an animal shelter. No matter how small, each action contributes to a ripple effect of positive change. Long-term commitments like sitting on a non-profit board can profoundly impact you and the community. It's about creating a legacy of service that inspires others to follow in your footsteps.

Finding the right volunteer opportunity is easier than ever, thanks to technology. Websites and apps dedicated to matching volunteers with opportunities abound, making it simple to find a cause that resonates with you. Platforms like United Way offer a range of options, from local to international projects. You can search based on your interests, location, and available time, ensuring a perfect fit. Remember to check out community bulletin boards or newsletters, which often list local volunteer needs. These resources are gold mines for discovering opportunities that might not be widely advertised but are highly rewarding.

Volunteering is about stepping out of your comfort zone and into a world where you can make a difference. It's an opportunity to engage with your community meaningfully, give back, and gain so much more in return. Whether planting trees, reading to children, or refurbishing community spaces, you're contributing to the world around you, one small act at a time. So, take that step, find a cause that speaks to you, and watch as it transforms your life and those you touch.

And as a bonus, it's a terrific way to meet and make new friends!

3.2 CREATING A SOCIAL CALENDAR: BALANCING SOLITUDE AND SOCIALIZING

Are you more of an introvert or an extrovert? It's a common misconception of those who know me that I thrive in the spotlight—truth be told, I'm an only child who cherishes solitude for its power to help me regroup and recharge. Yet, the beauty of our individuality lies in the balance; I find equal joy in the quiet of watching a baseball game at home and the vibrant energy of experiencing it live with my family among thousands. Recognizing and honoring our social preferences becomes crucial as we navigate the shift in our lives with our kids moving on.

Social interaction is more than just swapping stories over dinner. It's about the psychological benefits that come with those interactions. Studies have shown that social connections can boost our mood, increase our sense of belonging, and even keep our brains sharp as we age. It's like charging your social battery, one conversation at a time. But solitude has its perks, too. It allows us to reflect, recharge, and indulge in personal hobbies—like finding that last elusive puzzle piece. Solitude can be a time of creativity and introspection, where ideas flow freely, and your mind gets a break from the hustle and bustle. The trick is finding the right mix that suits your personality and lifestyle.

Planning a diverse social calendar can seem as daunting as organizing a family reunion, but it doesn't have to be. Start by scheduling regular meet-ups with friends or family. We talked about setting up ritual get-togethers, and we mentioned social groups. Not only do these provide regular social engagement, but they also offer a structured way to explore your interests. Plus, there's something comforting about knowing you'll see familiar faces regularly, sharing the joy of a good plot twist or a beautifully crafted scarf.

Remember to pencil in some alone time while filling your calendar with social events. This is your chance to indulge in self-care and reflection, a time to breathe and just be. Meditation or relaxation sessions can be the perfect antidote to a busy week. Imagine a quiet space with calming music, a place where you can let go of stress and reconnect with your inner self. Personal hobbies also play a crucial role in this solo time. Whether painting, writing, or gardening, these activities foster joy and creativity. They give you the freedom to express yourself without the pressure of an audience and a chance to explore new ideas and passions.

As life changes, so do our social needs. What worked for you last year might not fit this year. It's essential to remain flexible, adapting your social calendar as interests and circumstances evolve. This might mean re-evaluating social commitments periodically, like auditing your life for what sparks joy and what feels like a chore. It's okay to let go of activities that no longer serve you, making room for new experiences that align with your current interests. Perhaps you've discovered a newfound love for salsa dancing or have been intrigued by a local history club. Exploring new activities or groups can reinvigorate your social life, providing fresh perspectives and opportunities for growth.

In this dance of solitude and socializing, the key is listening to what you need each moment. Some days call for the company of friends, where laughter and conversation are the best medicine. On other days, a quiet stroll in the park with nothing but your thoughts for company can be just what the doctor ordered. Balancing these elements isn't about perfection; it's about creating a rhythm that feels right for you. So go ahead, build that social calendar with intention and heart, and watch as it enriches your life in ways you never imagined.

3.3 SUPPORT GROUPS: FINDING COMFORT IN SHARED EXPERIENCES

There's magic that happens when people come together over shared experiences. It's like finding the missing piece of a puzzle —a feeling of relief and connection that reminds you that you're not alone in this vast, sometimes overwhelming world. Do you think that you're the only empty nester out there? Support groups offer a kind of magic. They provide a space where you can share stories, laugh at the absurdities of life, and maybe even shed a tear or two without judgment. Whether you're dealing with an empty nest, managing a health issue, or navigating any other life challenge, there's likely a group ready to welcome you with open arms. These gatherings offer a sanctuary where you can be authentic, free from the masks we often wear daily.

Finding the right support group is a bit like dating. Try a few before you find the one that feels just right. Start by exploring online directories dedicated to support groups in your area. Websites like Meetup or Facebook can be invaluable resources, offering listings for everything from empty nester groups to those focused on mindfulness or career changes. Feel free to ask your healthcare provider or local community center for recommendations, as they often have insights into the best local options. Keep an open mind, and remember that attending a few meetings is okay before deciding if a group is the right fit for you.

Participating in a support group can be a transformative experience. People often find that sharing their stories with others who understand leads to profound personal growth. A unique kind of healing happens when you hear someone else articulate feelings you thought were only yours. It's like a light bulb flickering on, illuminating the shadows of doubt and loneliness. These groups provide a platform for exchanging advice, offering encouragement, and celebrating big and small successes. Personal testimonies abound of individuals who have found strength and resilience through the bonds formed in these circles. They speak of newfound confidence, clarity, and a sense of belonging that had been missing.

Creating or participating in a support group requires a commitment to fostering a safe, supportive environment. This means establishing guidelines for respectful and confidential interactions. It's crucial that members feel comfortable sharing their thoughts and feelings without fear of judgment or breach of privacy. Leadership roles within the group help facilitate this dynamic, ensuring that everyone's voice is heard and valued. These leaders, often volunteers, guide discussions, offer support, and help maintain a positive atmosphere. Their role is pivotal in creating a space where members can thrive, learning from one another in a spirit of collaboration and empathy.

Support groups are not just about facing challenges but about celebrating victories, too. They remind us that we're stronger together and that we can face life's ups and downs with courage when we have a tribe to lean on. As you navigate the empty nest phase, consider seeking a group that resonates with your needs.

These connections can enrich your life, offering friendship, understanding, and a sense of purpose. So, whether you're sharing stories over coffee or participating in a virtual discussion, remember that you're part of something bigger—a community here to support and uplift you.

As we wrap up this chapter on finding your people, remember that community is about more than just proximity. It's about shared experiences, mutual support, and the joy of connection. Whether you're joining a support group or volunteering for a cause, these interactions add color and richness to our lives. Now, as we move forward, let's revisit a topic we might have just forgotten about, even though it's been right in front of you the whole time.

4

HI BABE, REMEMBER ME?

My turn to share - I've been fortunate and blessed to be married to the mother of our children for 25+ years. If you've been married for that long, or you've made a big blended paradise along the way, I know a common question that pops up among us empty nesters: "Who is this person?"

Of course, it's not a question of forgetfulness; it's more like a reawakening to each other after years dedicated to our children. Jasmine and I had dreams and plans for this chapter of our lives, conversations that somehow got shelved as we focused on raising self-sufficient children. It's intriguing how those early dreams can feel distant, yet they're waiting to be rediscovered and realized. The empty nest phase can be a surprising second honeymoon if you play your cards right. So, dust off those dating skills and get ready to rediscover the partner you've shared your life with.

As life shifts, so do relationship needs. It's essential to reassess what both of you want from this new chapter. Maybe it's more adventure, like trying out that salsa class you never dared to attempt, or perhaps it's the simple pleasure of quiet evenings spent reading together. Consider hosting a relationship workshop or retreat for self-discovery. These can be enlightening experiences, offering new insights into each other's dreams and aspirations. If that sounds too formal, create a shared vision board at home. Grab some magazines, scissors, and glue, and let your imaginations run wild. It's a fun, creative way to visualize your goals and dreams, helping you align your future plans.

Rekindling romance isn't just about grand gestures; it's the small, everyday efforts that deepen intimacy. Start by scheduling uninterrupted time for conversations. In our busy lives, it's easy to let days slip by without a meaningful chat. Set aside regular times to connect without distractions—turn off the phones, dim the lights, and just talk. Explore new activities together, like taking a cooking class or revisiting hobbies you enjoyed in your early days. These shared experiences can reignite the spark and remind you why you were drawn to each other in the first place. Plus, they're fun and often lead to laughter, which is always a great bonding opportunity.

Of course, every relationship has its challenges. This transition can bring some to the forefront, but it's a chance to address them effectively. Conflict resolution workshops or resources can be beneficial, teaching valuable skills for navigating disagreements. Developing empathy through role-reversal exercises is another effective strategy. Try switching roles for a day to understand each other's perspectives better. This exercise can be eye-opening and often leads to greater compassion and understanding. Remember, challenges are not roadblocks but opportunities to grow stronger together.

Don't forget to celebrate the milestones that have brought you this far. Planning anniversary trips or special dinners is a beautiful way to honor your journey. These celebrations don't have to be extravagant. Sometimes, a picnic with a homemade meal in the park can be just as memorable. Creating a scrapbook of shared memories is another excellent way to reflect on your relationship's highlights. Include photos, mementos, and notes about the adventures and challenges you've faced together. It's a tangible reminder of the love and history you share, something you can look back on with pride and joy. Bonus - those kids you miss so much will be in those photos, too.

4.1 COMMUNICATION TECHNIQUES FOR DEEPER CONNECTION

Are you feeling a tension that you haven't felt before? It's normal for couples to struggle during this time. You might have found yourself sitting across from your partner, the room quiet except for the soft rustle of pages being turned. You're both there, in the same space, yet worlds apart. This isn't just physical distance; it's a gap in communication. Effective communication is the bridge that connects two people, allowing them to truly understand and support each other. It's like the secret sauce in any relationship—things can get pretty bland without it. Open and honest communication is all about being real with each other and sharing your thoughts and feelings without holding back. This requires active listening, which means being fully present, not just nodding while planning your next grocery list.

We always hear about communication, don't we? Big surprise - there's a reason for that! Communication is the key for you and your partner to be heard. Many times, empty nesters are in a period of depression, and sadly, that can carry right over to the way you treat the rest of the people in your life. A couple I met with that requested to be left anonymous told me that the first two weeks that their nest was empty were spent in tears, and the next couple months after that resulted in silence. This caused feelings of neglect and remorse -- you fill in the adjective, and you'd be right. Fortunately, this particular couple found salvation in counseling (hey, communication!) On the other hand, holding back communication can absolutely result in a pit of despair for your relationship, and worse case, absolutely lead to a breakup or divorce.

Improving communication skills is akin to sharpening a tool; it takes practice but pays off in spades. Start with "I feel" statements. Instead of pointing fingers with "You never listen," try "I feel unheard when…" It shifts the focus from blame to sharing personal experiences. Reflective listening practices can further enhance understanding. After your partner shares something, respond, "What I'm hearing is…" This confirms you're listening and opens the door for clarification. Remember, communication isn't just about words. Non-verbal cues like eye contact, facial expressions, and body language speak volumes. Being aware of these signals can prevent misunderstandings and foster empathy.

Expressing vulnerability in a relationship can be daunting, yet it's crucial for deepening bonds. It's about opening up those guarded corners of our hearts and trusting our partners with our innermost thoughts. To do this, create a safe space for sharing. This means agreeing to listen without judgment and offering support instead of solutions. Regular emotional check-ins can help maintain this safe space. These are dedicated times to share feelings, big or small, without the distractions of daily life. Imagine it like a pit stop in a race—essential for maintaining the health of your relationship.

Communication barriers are like potholes on a road trip. They can cause detours and delays if not addressed. Misunderstandings often arise from assumptions, so if something feels off, clarify before jumping to conclusions. A simple "Did you mean..." can avert many a misunderstanding. Avoiding defensive reactions is equally essential. When faced with criticism, try to respond with curiosity rather than defensiveness. It's about understanding the underlying needs and concerns rather than reacting to the surface message. These strategies can transform potential conflicts into opportunities for growth.

In the hustle of daily life and recent developments in the home, it's easy to let communication slip. But with a little effort, you can maintain that bridge, ensuring it stands firm against the winds of change. Effective communication is not just a skill; it's the heart of connection. It turns a house into a home, a partnership into a lifelong friendship. So, the next time you find yourself losing touch, remember the power of words, the magic they hold, and the love they can nurture. Have a conversation about communication - it sounds corny, but your partner is worth it, right?

4.2 FROM PLAYDATES TO DATE NIGHTS

Remember those days when your calendar was filled with playdates, birthday parties, and soccer games? With the kids out of the house, it's time to pencil in some quality time for just the two of you. Setting aside dedicated moments to reconnect can breathe new life into your relationship. Consider establishing a weekly date night. It doesn't have to be a grand affair. Sometimes, the best evenings are spent at home, whipping up a new recipe together. How about you don aprons, fumble through chopping vegetables, and laugh over a spilled sauce? It's not just about the meal but the shared experience and the stories that come with it. And if cooking isn't your thing, surprise each other with planned outings. Maybe one week, you choose a local art exhibit, and the next, your partner organizes a stargazing night. These surprises add excitement and anticipation, reminding you of the spontaneity that first brought you together.

Exploring new activities together can open doors to deeper connections. Outdoor adventures like hiking or biking get the endorphins flowing and provide the perfect backdrop for meaningful conversations. Imagine riding through a scenic trail, the wind in your hair, as you share thoughts and dreams with the person you've built a life with. Similarly, attending local cultural events or shows can offer a fresh perspective and a shared appreciation for the arts. These outings break the monotony and introduce elements of novelty to your routine. You might discover a mutual love for jazz or find yourselves debating the merits of modern art, sparking conversations that linger long after the event is over. It often inspires a new thought or venture that takes you through the rest of the day glowing.

Rediscovering shared interests can be a game-changer for your relationship. Remember the hobbies you enjoyed before life got hectic? Sounds like a fun weekend of rekindling fun. Of course, maintaining regular date nights can present challenges. Busy schedules, work commitments, and social obligations often compete for your time. To overcome these obstacles, consider time management strategies that prioritize your relationship. Block out date nights on your calendar as you would any necessary appointment. Rotating planning responsibilities can also relieve pressure and keep things fresh. You take the lead one week, and your partner does the next. This approach ensures that both partners are equally invested in maintaining the connection.

Balancing novelty with nostalgia adds a special touch to your time together. Recreate your first date or honeymoon, bringing back fond memories while adding your unique twist. Attend concerts of favorite bands from your youth, letting the music transport you to a time of carefree fun. These nostalgic experiences remind you of the journey you've taken together and the love that has grown through the years. At the same time, trying new things keeps the relationship vibrant and exciting, encouraging you both to step out of your comfort zones and embrace the unknown.

4.3 REINVENTING PARTNERSHIP ROLES

Once the kids have flown the coop, the dynamics at home shift in ways you might not expect. It's like the universe handed you a new playbook for life, and the rules are still being written. With the absence of children, suddenly the traditional roles you've held onto might need a little shaking up. The days of driving children to parties and juggling dinner are on the way out, and now it's about finding a new balance, like figuring out how to dance when the music changes. Sharing household responsibilities becomes a game of "Who can do it better?" rather than "Whose turn is it?" You might find yourself swapping roles—maybe one of you takes on the cooking while the other handles the finances. It's about discovering strengths you never knew you had and letting go of the ones you've outgrown. Balancing career and home life also takes on new meaning. Without the kids, there's a chance to reassess what matters most and perhaps even explore new professional avenues or hobbies that were previously sidelined.

But all this change can be a minefield without open dialogue. It's crucial to have a sit-down, the kind where you both lay your cards on the table—no poker faces allowed. Talking about your hopes and dreams is crucial, as assumptions can quietly undermine happiness. Think of scheduling regular check-ins as creating strategic planning sessions for your partnership. Choose a time, pour some coffee (or wine), and openly discuss successes, challenges, and future aspirations. This isn't about doling out tasks; it's about aligning on each other's needs and ambitions.

Creating an equitable partnership is like crafting a playlist for a long road trip—you need variety, balance, and a bit of compromise. Start by negotiating duties and tasks without the pressure of traditional gender roles. Maybe one of you is a whiz at DIY projects, while the other excels at planning getaways. Recognize each other's strengths and let them shine. This makes life smoother and ensures both partners feel valued and supported. It's about building a team where everyone plays to their strengths, turning the mundane into something a little more magical.

I've seen couples transform their partnerships in creative ways. Take the story of Alex and Francesca, who decided to swap roles for a month. Alex, who'd never cooked anything beyond toast, took over the kitchen while Francesca dove into the world of DIY repairs. It was a comedy of errors at first—Alex's burnt soufflés were legendary—but over time, they discovered hidden talents and developed newfound respect for each other's roles. It's heartening to see how role-swapping can breathe fresh air into relationships, teaching us that stepping into each other's shoes can be both enlightening and hilarious.

Reinventing partnership roles is about evolution, not revolution. It's a chance to shake up the status quo and redefine what works for you now. This phase of life is an open invitation to rewrite the rules, find joy in the unexpected, and laugh at the missteps along the way.

4.4 FACING THE FEAR OF AGING TOGETHER

Fear is a monster, and its minions work hard against you daily - especially now. Combine fear in a toxic potion with the concept of aging, and well - aging is like an uninvited guest at a party, inevitable and often greeted with mixed emotions. As you and your partner navigate this phase together, it's easy to find yourselves staring into the mirror, noticing the silver that wasn't there last year, pondering those creaky joints, and questioning where the time has gone. These physical changes and the looming health issues can stir up fears that sometimes feel too big to voice. Conversations about these fears might seem daunting, but they're crucial. Think of them as the foundation for addressing the changes ahead. Speaking openly about what makes you anxious can transform those worries from insurmountable mountains into manageable hills. Maybe it's the fear of losing independence or the uncertainty of health challenges. Whatever the concern, acknowledging it can be the first step toward acceptance.

Embracing aging with optimism is more than just a mindset—it's a lifestyle choice. Celebrate those life milestones with gusto! Each birthday, anniversary, and achievement is a testament to the life you've built together. Why not throw a party for the little things, like conquering a new hobby or finishing a book? These celebrations aren't just about marking time; they're about honoring the journey and the shared achievements that have brought you this far. Focusing on what's been accomplished together shifts the narrative from one of loss to one of gratitude and fulfillment. These shared moments become stories you'll tell over and over, each one a thread in the fabric of your relationship.

Planning for the future isn't just about dreaming—it's about preparing. Consider sitting down together to create a health and wellness plan that suits both of you. Perhaps it involves joining a fitness class or adopting a new eating plan to boost energy and vitality. It's about making choices today that pave the way for a healthier tomorrow. Discussing future lifestyle choices can be empowering, transforming what could be a source of anxiety into a proactive partnership. Explore options for staying active and engaged, ensuring that you're both on the same page. It's not just about longevity; it's about quality of life. These plans become a shared commitment, a promise to face whatever comes hand in hand.

Inspiration can be found in couples who have navigated aging with grace and humor. Take, for instance, Emily and Frank, a couple who embraced retirement with a zest for life that was infectious. They swapped city living for a small cottage by the sea, spending their days exploring new hobbies and volunteering at the local community center. Their story isn't about escape; it's about intentional living. They found joy in the simple things—morning walks along the shore, cooking meals together, and hosting game nights for friends. Their journey reminds us that aging can be a time of exploration and deep connection. It's a chance to revisit the passions that life's busyness sometimes pushes aside and to rediscover each other in the warmth of shared experiences.

Can't sell everything and move to an island? We can still find happiness together in our daily tasks. All of a sudden, that dessert that you used to rush together and was gobbled down like a hungry hurricane is now available to you to eat at your leisure. No wonder they used to love this dish! Visiting the same park with your partner like you did for years with your children somehow seems a lot bigger and brighter now. We spent so much time on the playground that we had no idea there was a beautiful walking path just paces away! It's so odd that a world that seemed so closed just weeks before could feel more open than it ever was!

Don't let fear hold you back. Fear was the fuel for so many outstanding achievements in this world, and it might just power you past your obstacles, too.

4.5 PLANNING A LEGACY TOGETHER

Legacy in a relationship is like planting a tree whose shade you'll never sit under. It's about creating something lasting that reflects who you are as a couple and what you stand for. This isn't just about leaving behind a financial inheritance; it's about the values, traditions, and memories that define your partnership. To get started, think about what personal and shared legacies mean to you. Maybe it's a family tradition you've built over the years or a shared passion for community service. Whatever it is, defining these legacies can offer a sense of purpose and direction. It's a way to ensure that the love and commitment you've nurtured continue to flourish, even as the years roll by.

Glen is a 50-year-old empty nester, and after evaluating his legacy to this world beyond being a great dad, he decided to undertake the steps to redefine what he was in the eyes of his world. That could be anything to anyone - to Glen, it was to start a non-profit organization for animal rescue. His partner, Emily, holds a degree in marketing and business, and this new vision helped them create a new bond.

Setting shared long-term goals is a crucial step in legacy-building. These goals should reflect your values and aspirations, creating a roadmap for the future you both envision. Start by sitting down together, perhaps over a pot of coffee or a bottle of wine, and draft a shared vision board. This isn't about being artistic; it's about visualizing your dreams and setting intentions. Cut out images and words that resonate with your shared goals, whether it's traveling to a new country every year or starting a family business. This vision board becomes a tangible reminder of what you're working towards and keeps you focused on the path ahead. By aligning your goals, you strengthen the bond and create a partnership that's united in purpose.

Building a legacy isn't just about setting goals; it's about taking action. Consider engaging in legacy-building activities that leave a lasting impact on your community and family. Volunteering for a cause you both care about is a powerful way to give back and make a difference. It could be anything from mentoring young people to participating in environmental conservation efforts. The key is to find something that ignites a shared passion and allows you to contribute positively to the world around you. Establishing family traditions is another meaningful way to build a legacy. These could be annual family reunions, holiday rituals, or even a simple weekly dinner that brings everyone together. These traditions create a sense of belonging and continuity, passing down cherished memories to future generations.

Working towards a common purpose has countless benefits. It strengthens the partnership, creating a sense of unity and fulfillment. When you achieve goals together, there's a shared sense of accomplishment that reinforces your bond. Celebrate these achievements, whether it's completing a volunteer project or reaching a personal milestone. Throw a little party, take a trip, or simply share a quiet moment of gratitude. These celebrations aren't just about marking progress; they're about acknowledging the hard work and dedication you've put into building a life together. They remind you of what you've achieved and keep the momentum going as you continue to pursue your dreams.

As we wrap up this chapter on planning a legacy together, remember that legacy-building is an ongoing process. It evolves as you grow and change, adapting to new experiences and challenges. It's a dynamic, living testament to the love and commitment you share. As you continue to work towards these shared goals, you create a partnership that's rich in purpose and meaning.

5

FLYING SOLO - WHERE DID EVERYONE GO?

In doing my research for this chapter, I relied heavily on listening to stories from friends who are single parents. I heard a lot of similar voices -- lack of purpose, depression, aloneness. But the depth of that darkness was amplified as a single parent. My heart went out to friends I spoke to, and each person made sure to tell me it was a daily work in progress. My mother was a single parent. She seemed to always be busy trying to string together finances and constantly working to put me first above everything. For 18 years, I was absolutely her life. When I flew the nest and started writing my own story, I didn't think much about how my mom would be affected. I think about it now, that's for sure!

It's an odd sensation, realizing that the busy symphony of everyday life has quieted down to a solo performance. But here's the twist: solitude doesn't have to be a lonely affair. It's a chance to rediscover yourself, like finding an old record at the back of your collection and remembering why you loved it. And surprise, a lot of the techniques for couples can be worked right into the world of the single parent.

Solitude can be a powerful tool for self-discovery, especially for single parents who might be used to juggling more roles than a circus performer. It's time to shift the narrative from solitude as isolation to solitude as empowerment. Think of it as a chance to uncover the parts of yourself that were put on hold. Start by reframing solitude into something positive. Instead of seeing it as a void, view it as a stage set for exploring your passions and dreams. Grab a journal and jot down your personal strengths. What are you good at? What makes you tick? This process is like giving yourself a pep talk without the awkwardness of talking to your reflection. Writing it down boosts your self-esteem and provides a tangible list of what makes you unique and capable.

Now that you're starting to view solitude as your ally, it's time to enjoy it. Plan solo adventures that put a spring in your step. Whether hiking in the local park, visiting a museum, or simply strolling through the farmer's market, these outings are about embracing your independence. Solo hobbies can also bring immense joy—think gardening, painting, or even learning to play an instrument. These activities are like gifts you give yourself, providing fulfillment and a sense of accomplishment. They're opportunities to immerse yourself in something you love without needing anyone else's approval.

Embracing self-reliance is another step toward personal growth. Setting personal goals without external validation can be freeing. It's about finding what you want to achieve for yourself, unshackled by others' expectations. Maybe you've wanted to learn a new language, take up yoga, or write that novel. These goals are yours to pursue, and the satisfaction comes from knowing you're doing it for you. It's a journey of resilience, learning to rely on your strengths and instincts.

To bolster your self-confidence, engage in exercises that reinforce your self-worth. Daily affirmations can work wonders. Stand in front of the mirror and repeat positive statements about yourself. Sure, it might feel silly at first, but words have power. Reflective exercises are also invaluable; think back on past achievements, no matter how small. Perhaps you tackled a challenging project at work or learned a new skill. Recognizing these victories reminds you of your capabilities and builds a foundation of confidence to take on new challenges.

5.1 DEALING WITH GUILT OR WORRY

As a single parent, you've carried the weight of being both the primary caregiver and the main source of support for your children. Now that they've left the nest, it's only natural for feelings of guilt or worry to surface. You might find yourself questioning whether you did enough to prepare them for life on their own or whether certain decisions you made along the way were the right ones. These lingering doubts can sometimes overshadow your pride in seeing them grow into independent adults.

After Jennifer's divorce, she poured everything into raising her daughter, Mia. The end of her marriage was painful, but Jennifer pushed through, determined to give Mia a stable life. Over the years, they became a strong team, and Jennifer found comfort in their routine. But when Mia left for college, Jennifer was hit by a new wave of loneliness. Without Mia at home, the grief of the divorce resurfaced, and the silence felt overwhelming. It was as if she were facing her loss all over again. She even started doubting herself and if she really had done everything she could have done for Mia.

It's important to acknowledge that guilt and worry are expected during this transition and to remind yourself that no parent, single or otherwise, is perfect. You've done your best under the circumstances, often balancing financial, emotional, and practical responsibilities on your own. Jennifer would benefit from this. Rather than letting these feelings consume you, try reframing your perspective: instead of asking, "Did I do enough?" focus on what you've accomplished and how your efforts have shaped your children into capable, resilient individuals. Trust in the foundation you've laid and allow yourself to let go of some of that worry, knowing that the skills and values you've instilled in them will guide them forward. I realize that we are their biggest fan, but it's pretty easy to step back and see what you've done here! Are they learning a new trade or studying hard in school? Maybe they're already working to better their life and sustain themselves? Fantastic! Take the energy you're putting into feeling down and channel that into a pat on the back. There's a lot to be proud of!

Interactive Element: Reflective Exercise

1. **What losses are you grieving in this new chapter?** (Identify what you feel you've lost, whether it's your role as a full-time parent, daily routines, or a sense of purpose.)
2. **In what ways have you grown stronger through this experience?** (Reflect on how you've handled challenges as a single parent and how those strengths can help you now.)
3. **What are some things you're proud of accomplishing as a single parent?** (List moments or milestones that highlight your resilience and capability, even during difficult times.)
4. **How can you turn this grief into an opportunity for self-growth?** (Think about how this experience, while painful, might help you rediscover your passions, set new goals, or focus on yourself in a positive way.)
5. **What steps can you take to rebuild your confidence moving forward?** (Write down small, actionable steps to help you regain confidence, such as starting a new hobby, reaching out to old friends, or learning something new.)

5.2 FINANCIAL PLANNING FOR SINGLE PARENTS

My friends often ponder the unique financial tightrope that single parents walk. Balancing the budget can feel like juggling flaming swords while riding a unicycle. It's a challenge, no doubt, but it's not insurmountable. And while let's face it, our children will most likely continue to occasionally view us as a bright, shiny piggy bank, there's some room here to expand how we think about money as a single unit in the household.

The first step is creating a comprehensive budget plan. Think of it as your financial GPS, guiding you through the maze of bills, groceries, and unexpected expenses. Start by listing all sources of income and financial obligations, separating needs from wants. Now that your trips to Costco will be much lighter (or even unnecessary), what are our new needs and wants? Prioritize expenses to ensure essentials are covered, and consider building an emergency fund—a financial cushion for those unexpected hiccups life throws your way. It's like having a financial umbrella for those rainy days.

Managing finances effectively is the key to navigating this landscape. Reducing household expenses we don't need anymore can make a significant difference. Or maybe we want to start saving up for a trip? Consider the following expenses that you might not have realized that may be disappearing or changing:

- Housing Costs (Do you still need three bedrooms? Opportunity to rent out spaces? Downsize?)
- Food and Grocery Bills (fewer bulk items and food in general. Teenagers can eat!)
- Transportation (multiple cars for commuting kids to school or activities)
- Education (private school expenses no more? Extracurricular, tutoring, school supplies)
- Insurance policies (some can be adjusted for dependents)
- Subscriptions and entertainment (Are we really going to be watching Disney+ anymore?)

Financial planning also means increasing your budget for interests you couldn't make room for before. Have you ever wanted to go organic at the market? Home delivery of fresh fruits and vegetables? Perhaps now these are possibilities.

You've heard time is money - another strategy is increasing your income. Side gigs or freelance work can provide a financial boost without needing a full-time commitment. Platforms like Upwork or Fiverr offer opportunities to monetize skills you might already have. Consider teaching a class, offering consultancy, or even selling crafts online. It's about finding and making the most of what works for you.

Financial literacy is your secret weapon. It's not just about balancing checkbooks or deciphering tax codes, though that's part of it. It's about understanding how money works and using that knowledge to make informed decisions. Resources for financial education are plentiful. Websites like InCharge.org or local community colleges offer workshops and courses on budgeting, investing, and debt management. These are invaluable in empowering you to take charge of your financial future. Think of it like learning a new language—financial fluency opens doors to opportunities and security. The more you know, the better equipped you are to tackle financial challenges.

Long-term financial planning is essential. Consider investment options tailored for single parents. There might be some extra money to invest in your and your children's future. Retirement planning should also be a priority. Explore strategies like IRAs or 401(k) plans, taking advantage of employer-matched contributions. It's about setting yourself up for a comfortable and secure future. Start by consulting a financial advisor if needed. They can provide tailored advice and strategies that align with your goals. Regularly reviewing and adjusting your plan ensures it remains realistic and aligned with any changes in your financial situation.

Financial planning doesn't have to be daunting. It's about taking small, consistent steps towards security and stability. It's about making informed choices that align with your life goals.

As you navigate this path, remember that you're not alone. There are resources, tools, and communities ready to support you.

5.3 COPING WITH LONELINESS: PRACTICAL TIPS

Loneliness can sneak up on you like a cat looking for a warm lap. One minute, you're fine; the next, you wonder why the silence is so loud. It's a reality many single parents face, even though it's not always easy to admit. I wasn't a single parent, but I sure felt like one when my spouse was working a weekend, and it was just the dogs and me. But it's okay to feel lonely sometimes. In fact, acknowledging it is the first step toward finding a solution. My friend Rosy experienced this. She moved to a new city after her divorce, her kids spent every other week with their dad, and she found herself alone on those quiet evenings. She felt like she was the only person on a deserted island. But instead of wallowing, she decided to turn things around.

One of the most effective strategies she found was volunteering. It's incredible how giving your time to others can fill your own cup. Whether helping at a local shelter or joining a community garden project, volunteering connects you with others and gives you a sense of purpose. Plus, you get to meet people who share your values and passions. Rosy also joined a pottery class, a childhood interest she had always wanted to explore. It wasn't just about learning a new skill; it was about being part of a group, sharing laughs over misshapen bowls, and feeling a sense of belonging. Group activities or classes are perfect opportunities to meet new people and build connections that can ease loneliness.

Self-compassion also plays a significant role in coping with loneliness. It involves treating yourself with the same kindness you'd offer a friend. When those lonely feelings creep in, it's easy to be hard on yourself. But instead, try to practice self-compassion. Take a moment to acknowledge your feelings without judgment. Self-compassion exercises can be simple yet powerful. Start with a few deep breaths, place your hand over your heart, and remind yourself that feeling this way is okay. You are not alone, and these feelings will pass. It's about being gentle with yourself, recognizing your worth, and understanding that you deserve kindness from yourself as much as from others.

It's also important to know where to turn for additional support. Sometimes, you need more than just a chat with a friend. That's where helplines and community resources come into play. They offer a listening ear and practical advice. Organizations like CoAbode provide support specifically for single parents, offering resources and community connections. Additionally, mental health support through therapy or counseling can provide a safe space to explore your feelings and develop strategies to combat loneliness. These resources are invaluable, offering guidance and companionship when you need it most. They remind you that you are part of a larger community that's ready to lend a hand when the going gets tough.

Navigating loneliness is a bit like finding your way through a foggy forest. The path isn't always clear, but with the right tools and support, you can find your way to brighter days. Whether it's through volunteering, joining a class, or practicing self-kindness, each step you take brings you closer to a more connected and fulfilling life.

5.4 NAVIGATING NEW RELATIONSHIPS POST-NEST

Entering the dating world as a single parent can feel like stepping onto a rollercoaster you haven't ridden in a while. It's thrilling, a bit nerve-wracking, and you're not entirely sure where it will lead. After years of focusing on your kids, you suddenly have the opportunity to focus on yourself and what you want in a partner. It's a mixed bag of emotions, from excitement to apprehension. The dynamics are different now. You're not just dating as you but as you-plus-family. Understanding your personal readiness is critical. Ask yourself if you're truly ready to welcome someone new into your life. It's okay to take your time. The right moment doesn't have to be rushed. When you feel ready, it's essential to approach this new chapter with an open heart and mind.

Janet lost her husband, Todd, when their children were just 8 and 10. She focused solely on raising them for years, leaving little time to think about her own life. But as her children grew up and moved out, the once-busy house became quiet. For the first time in a long while, Janet found herself wondering what came next for her. The thought of dating again felt strange and guilt-laden. Was she betraying Todd by even considering it? Would her children understand? But over time, Janet realized that wanting companionship didn't mean she loved her late husband any less. It simply meant she was ready to rediscover her own happiness. Slowly, she dipped her toes back into dating—meeting new people over coffee, having casual conversations. It wasn't easy, but it was a step toward embracing this new chapter of her life. Janet realized that her heart still had room for love. Now, she's learning that moving forward doesn't erase the past but opens the door to new possibilities.

Building healthy relationships starts with setting boundaries. These boundaries aren't walls to keep people out but rather guidelines that protect your well-being and ensure mutual respect. Be clear about your comfort and communicate your needs early on. This establishes a foundation of trust and respect. Effective communication with new partners is vital. It's about expressing your thoughts and feelings honestly while being open to theirs. Remember, you're both navigating these waters, so patience and understanding go a long way. Discuss expectations and be upfront about your situation, whether it's co-parenting commitments or work schedules. This transparency helps avoid misunderstandings and builds a stronger connection.

While dating, it's crucial to maintain your independence and personal identity. The temptation to lose oneself in a relationship is real, but balancing your own needs with the dynamics of dating ensures you stay grounded. Make time for your interests and passions. This enriches your life and brings vibrancy to the relationship. A partner should complement your life, not complete it. It's about being two whole individuals who choose to share their journeys. Balancing personal needs with relationship dynamics means carving out space for yourself and ensuring you don't neglect the things that make you unique.

There are countless stories of single parents finding fulfilling relationships that bring joy and growth. Take Evelyn, for example. After years of being single, she met Tom at a local community event. They bonded over shared interests and a love for adventure. Their connection was built on mutual respect and understanding, valuing the other's independence. Or consider Mike, who found companionship with Anne through a mutual friend. They both had kids and understood the complexities of blending families. Their relationship blossomed as they supported each other's roles as parents while nurturing their partnership. These stories highlight the possibilities that await when you open yourself to new connections.

As we close this chapter, remember that love doesn't come with a script. It's an unscripted dance with its own rhythm. Embrace the opportunities that come your way, and let them unfold naturally. There's no rush, no timeline, just the beautiful unfolding of what's meant to be. As we turn the page, we'll explore what lies beyond the nest, embracing the unknown with open arms.

UNLOCK THE POWER OF SHARING YOUR EXPERIENCE

> *"We make a living by what we get, but we make a life by what we give."*
>
> — WINSTON CHURCHILL

The best thing about learning is passing it on to others who need it, just like you did. If you've felt encouraged or inspired by *Filling the Empty Nest,* I'd love your help to make a difference for someone else.

Would you help another parent, curious and maybe even nervous about navigating the empty nest, by sharing your thoughts?

My goal with this book is to help make the empty nest transition a time of rediscovery and joy for as many people as possible. But to reach more parents on this journey, I need your support. Most people choose books based on the honest words of others. Your review could guide a fellow empty nester, offering encouragement and showing them they're not alone.

Taking just a minute to leave an honest review costs nothing but could change someone's entire experience.

Your review could:

- ...give other parents confidence in the transition ahead.
- ...inspire someone to embrace this new chapter with joy.
- ...connect another parent to a community of support and ideas.
- ...turn curiosity into courage for one more reader.

If you'd like to help make a difference, simply scan the QR code below and share your thoughts. Thank you for being part of this journey!

With immense gratitude, Rick Baptist

6

THE ROLE REVERSAL - PARENTING YOUR PARENTS

Often, newly discovered hours in the day can be filled with self-improvement and new adventures. But for many of us, those new blocks of time freedom end up getting filled pretty quickly when we realize our parents need help.

According to data from the Bureau of Labor Statistics, around 16% of Americans provide unpaid care to adults aged 65 or older. That's a lot of you who are somewhere between uneasy and gracious to devote time to your parents and wondering what happened to all this free time (and money) you envisioned having from the empty nest.

Remember my mom, who was left at home while I went off and spread my wings? So many of us have a learned or acquired need to care for others. It makes sense since we identify so strongly as parents. Our kids aren't just some houseplant that we water once a week! So now, instead of focusing 50/50 on raising me and taking care of Grandma, there was a dramatic shift to take over 100% on caregiving for her mother. As rewarding as taking care of an elderly parent can be, it can absolutely take over your life and set you up for yet again another empty nest in the near future.

When I'm not writing books, I've had a career spanning over 15 years supporting seniors and their families. My roles have ranged from serving in an elder law firm to working in assisted living and memory care facilities. Presently, I am a senior advisor, where I share critical insight and guidance with families navigating the complexities of elder care. Over the years, I can tell you that this situation is becoming more common. Long-term care costs are not decreasing, so family involvement in elder care is sorely needed. It's a topic that entirely needs to be addressed here as there might be another egg for our nest coming sooner rather than later.

6.1 OUR SECOND SHIFT

After the kids leave, many empty nesters think they're done with caregiving. But for some, a new, unexpected responsibility is waiting: caring for an elderly parent. This transition can feel like stepping right back into a familiar role but with an entirely different dynamic. Instead of carpooling and soccer games, it's medical appointments and ensuring prescriptions are filled. It's as if the "nest" you thought was finally empty is quickly filled again, only with different and unfamiliar tasks. It can be overwhelming on several levels - from financial to time restraints to maintaining parent/child dignity. You might be wondering how you're going to be able to get back in the saddle again.

When Rebecca's youngest son left for college, she finally could focus on herself. After years of packed schedules and soccer practices, her home was quiet, and she had big plans to travel and explore new hobbies. But just a few months later, her mother's health began to decline rapidly. The independence Rebecca thought she'd gained was quickly replaced by a new set of responsibilities—doctor appointments, medication management, and daily care for her aging mother.

At first, Rebecca struggled to accept this unexpected shift. She felt guilty for resenting her new role and overwhelmed by the demands of caregiving. But slowly, she found her rhythm. She realized that, like raising her children, caring for her mother required patience and love. Rebecca learned to find moments of joy in their time together, from quiet conversations to revisiting old family stories. Though the "empty nest" phase she envisioned had been postponed, Rebecca discovered a deeper connection with her mother and a new appreciation for the strength within herself.

You might share some similarities with Rebecca, or perhaps you're at the "resenting and overwhelmed" stage. Well, we have to start somewhere, don't we?

6.2 THE EMOTIONAL IMPACT

There's a unique emotional complexity that comes with this shift. On one hand, it can feel like you're fulfilling a natural duty—after all, your parents once cared for you. On the other hand, you might catch yourself feeling frustrated or even cheated, as if your newfound freedom has been replaced by another form of caregiving. This rollercoaster of emotions can bring back the same feelings of attachment and loss you thought you'd left behind when your kids moved out.

Focusing on caring for an aging parent gives you something tangible to invest your time and energy into, but it doesn't erase the underlying feelings. In many ways, you're filling one gap with another, delaying the inevitable realization that you'll soon face another empty nest when your parent is no longer there to care for.

It's essential to acknowledge that caring for an elderly parent often leads to yet another loss—the loss of the parent. When that moment arrives, it can feel like experiencing the empty nest all over again, but with deeper layers of grief and reflection. You've gone from being a caretaker for your children to a caretaker for your parent, and now, you're left with no one to look after, which can feel profoundly disorienting.

While caregiving can feel like a perpetual cycle, it's important to start thinking about how you'll reclaim your life after this second empty nest. Rather than being defined by your roles as a parent or caregiver, this period can offer the opportunity to redefine who you are. It's time to prioritize self-care and create space for your own needs, passions, and desires—because the one person you'll always have to care for is yourself.

Reflective Exercise: Understanding Your Emotions in Your New Role

1. **What emotions have surfaced since taking on the role of caregiver?** (Write down any feelings that have come up—such as frustration, sadness, guilt, or even joy—and reflect on how these emotions have impacted your day-to-day life.)
2. **How do you feel about the role reversal between you and your parent?** (Explore your thoughts on the shift in dynamics. Do you find it hard to care for the person who once cared for you? What emotions does this reversal bring up for you?)
3. **What challenges are you facing in this new role?** (Consider the practical and emotional challenges you've encountered so far. Are there any aspects that feel particularly difficult or overwhelming?)
4. **How do you balance your feelings of responsibility with your need for boundaries?** (Reflect on how you're managing the responsibility of caregiving while maintaining boundaries for your own well-being. What boundaries, if any, do you need to set for yourself?)
5. **What are you proud of in this caregiving journey so far?** (List any moments or aspects of caregiving that make you feel proud or fulfilled. Acknowledging these can help you see the positive aspects of this challenging role.)
6. **Reflective Exercise: Moving Forward in Your Caregiving Role**
   1. **How do you want to grow in this role?** (Think about how you might want to improve your caregiving skills or how you want to grow emotionally through this experience.)

2. **What support do you need?** (Reflect on where you could use help—whether from family, friends, or professional caregivers—and how reaching out might improve your experience and reduce stress.)
3. **How has this experience shaped your relationship with your parent?** (Consider how caregiving has changed your relationship with your parent. What new dynamics have emerged, and how have you both adapted?)

6.3 THE PRACTICAL SIDE OF CAREGIVING

While the emotional toll of caregiving is significant, the day-to-day logistics can also be overwhelming. From managing medical appointments and medication schedules to coordinating with other family members and ensuring your parent's safety, caregiving comes with a long list of tasks that can quickly pile up.

Developing efficient systems is crucial for managing the myriad tasks that come with caregiving. Start by creating a shared digital calendar accessible to all involved family members, where you can schedule and update doctor's appointments in real-time. Utilize smartphone reminders or set up a dedicated medication app to keep track of dosages and refill times, ensuring you never miss a beat. Embrace the power of technology to simplify these processes. Consider exploring services that offer automated prescription refills, or apps specifically designed to monitor your parent's health and well-being. Integrating these tools into your caregiving routine can significantly reduce the administrative burden and focus more on the personal aspects of care.

Additionally, consider talking to your parent about legal and financial planning. While these conversations can be difficult, having clear directives on issues like power of attorney, living wills, and financial management will help ease future decisions. The earlier you begin these discussions, the less stressful they'll be when a crisis arises. Being proactive about these logistical issues can lighten your mental load and give you more time to focus on your emotional health.

Another key aspect of the practical side of caregiving is understanding and utilizing available resources. Many caregivers don't realize there is support out there, from government programs to community services. Look into resources like Medicare, Medicaid, and local senior care programs that may offer assistance with medical expenses, in-home care, or respite care. Connecting with organizations like the AARP or elder care support groups can provide valuable advice and access to tools that help streamline your caregiving duties. It's easy to feel like you must handle everything independently, but tapping into these resources can lighten your load and ensure your parent receives the best possible care. Taking the time to explore these options will not only save time and money but also provide peace of mind as you navigate this new chapter.

6.4 SETTING BOUNDARIES AND MAINTAINING YOUR IDENTITY

As you step into the role of caregiver for your parent, it's easy to lose sight of your own needs and identity. The constant demands make it feel like there's little room left for yourself. However, it's crucial to establish boundaries—not just with your parent but also with yourself—so that caregiving doesn't consume every part of your life.

Boundaries can be as simple as setting aside a specific time each day for your activities, such as reading, exercise, or hobbies. Or it might mean having an honest conversation with your parent about when you need personal time. You've already spent years raising your children, and now that your nest is empty again, it's essential to nurture your own growth and goals, too. Let's not forget about all those juicy ideas in previous chapters!

Maintaining your identity is about recognizing that you are more than just a caregiver. You still have passions, ambitions, and a life that deserves attention. Don't be afraid to invest in yourself, even in small ways, while you care for your parent.

Reflective Exercise: Reclaiming Your Time and Space

- What boundaries do you need to set in your caregiving role to preserve your own well-being?
- How can you start prioritizing activities or hobbies that give you joy?
- What steps can you take to maintain your identity outside of being a caregiver?

7

CHILL OUT! MENTAL WELLNESS VIBES

We've gotten this far together, and we all likely have some emotional baggage weighing us down right now. Maybe you're reading this book to prepare yourself for the journey to come? Either way, this chapter is a reminder that mental wellness is something all of us can benefit from every day, every minute. So, with you and your nest in mind, consider these wonderful ideas to clear your head and move forward in your day!

7.1 JOURNALING FOR JOY

Picture this: you're sitting on your couch with a cup of tea, the kind that promises to calm nerves and soothe the soul. The house is quiet, save for the soft ticking of the clock and the occasional rustle of leaves outside. In this serene moment, you might find yourself reflecting on the whirlwind that life has been. Kids have flown the coop, and now it's just you, your thoughts, and an open notebook staring back at you. Welcome to the world of journaling—a space where you can spill your thoughts without judgment and maybe even find some clarity amidst the chaos. It's a bit like having a conversation with yourself, only you get to decide when the discussion ends.

Journaling is more than just putting pen to paper; it's a powerful tool for emotional expression and reflection. Studies show that journaling can significantly improve mental health by helping to process negative thoughts and emotions. According to research from Psych Central, consistent journaling has been linked to reduced anxiety and increased resilience, making it an effective self-care technique. It's like a mental detox, where you can vent, reflect, and even discover insights you didn't know you had. Some people find transformation through journaling, like my friend Mike, who started journaling during a particularly stressful period. Through his entries, he realized he'd been holding onto fears that weren't serving him. By the end of his journaling journey, Mike's pages were filled with not only his worries but also his hopes and dreams, giving him a more straightforward path forward.

To harness the benefits of journaling, consider various techniques to gain clarity on your feelings and experiences. Stream-of-consciousness writing is an excellent method for unfiltered expression. It's like letting your mind wander freely, capturing thoughts as they come without overthinking or editing. This technique can unearth hidden emotions and help you make sense of them. Gratitude journaling, on the other hand, focuses on the positive aspects of your life. By jotting down things you're grateful for, you shift your focus from what's lacking to what's abundant. Finally, prompt-based journaling provides structure for those who might feel lost staring at a blank page. Prompts such as "What do I need right now?" or "What's one thing I've learned recently?" can guide your reflections and spark meaningful insights.

Establishing a consistent journaling practice can be a game-changer, like finding the perfect morning routine that sets the tone for your day. Start by dedicating a specific time and place for journaling, whether first thing in the morning, during your lunch break, or before bed. Create a cozy nook with your favorite chair, a soft blanket, and perhaps a candle or two. Choose the right tools that make journaling enjoyable—some prefer the tactile feel of traditional notebooks, while others opt for digital apps that sync across devices. The goal is to make journaling a habit, a sacred ritual that allows you to pause, reflect, and recharge.

Reflecting on past entries is an opportunity to recognize personal growth and change. It's like flipping through a photo album of your inner world, seeing how much you've evolved. Analyze your journal entries for recurring themes or patterns. Are there specific triggers that consistently appear? How have your responses changed? Summarizing lessons learned can provide valuable insights and guide future actions. Consider creating a summary or list of key takeaways from your journaling journey. This reflection highlights your progress and reinforces the positive changes you've made. It's a reminder that you're moving forward, one entry at a time, despite the ups and downs.

Interactive Element: Journaling Prompts for Emotional Clarity

1. Write about a moment that brought you unexpected joy this week.
2. What is something you're grateful for today, and why?
3. Describe a challenge you're currently facing and how you feel about it.
4. Reflect on a recent success and the steps you took to achieve it.
5. List three things you love about yourself that have nothing to do with your roles.

Journaling is a personal journey, one that offers a window into your soul, allowing you to explore, understand, and embrace the complexities of life. It's a tool for healing, growth, and self-discovery that's always available and ready to listen. So, grab that notebook, find your favorite pen, and just go for it!

7.2 MINDFULNESS PRACTICES FOR BALANCE AND PEACE

Mindfulness is the new buzzword that has seemed to creep into our everyday language overnight. It's not new by any means. Rooted in ancient Eastern practices, mindfulness has been around for centuries, offering a way to focus on the present moment with intention and awareness. But here's the twist—it's not just meditation. Mindfulness is about being fully present in whatever you're doing, whether that's washing dishes or raking the leaves. It's the art of living in the now, which can be a lifesaver when you're feeling pulled in a thousand directions.

Incorporating mindfulness into daily life doesn't require a trip to a mountaintop or a silent retreat. You can start with simple techniques that seamlessly fit into your routine. Take body scan exercises, for example. These invite you to focus on each part of your body, noticing sensations without judgment. It's like giving yourself a mental check-up, allowing you to identify and release areas of tension. Then there's mindful breathing, a technique that's as simple as it sounds. Taking slow, deep breaths can calm your mind and reduce stress, almost like hitting the pause button on your thoughts. And don't forget about walking meditation. This isn't your typical stroll in the park. It's about being aware of each step, the sensation of your feet touching the ground, and the rhythm of your movement. These practices can transform mundane moments into opportunities for peace and clarity.

The benefits of mindfulness extend beyond just feeling zen. Research has shown that mindfulness can significantly reduce stress and enhance emotional well-being. Jessica found herself drowning in work and family obligations. She decided to give mindfulness a shot, starting with just five minutes daily. Initially skeptical, she soon noticed a shift. Her stress levels dropped, and she felt more in control. Studies back this up, showing that mindfulness can decrease cortisol levels—the pesky stress hormone—and improve overall health. It's shocking that just a few minutes of intentional focus leads to a cascade of positive effects. It's like finding a hidden superpower within yourself.

Creating a mindful environment at home is another step in embracing this practice. Picture your dream space for relaxation—a corner of your home that invites calm and reflection. Designing a meditation corner doesn't have to be elaborate. A comfortable chair, a soft cushion, and a small plant can transform a nook into your personal sanctuary. Consider adding calming scents like lavender or chamomile to enhance your mindfulness practice. Sound plays a role, too. Gentle music or nature sounds can drown out distractions and help center your thoughts. It's all about crafting a space that feels like a retreat, even if it's just a corner of your living room. You might have an empty bedroom or three?

Interactive Element: Creating Your Mindful Space

1. **Choose Your Spot**: Find a quiet corner in your home with minimal distractions. This will be your designated mindfulness area.
2. **Comfort is Key**: Select a cozy chair or cushion to sit on. Your comfort will allow you to focus on your practice without physical discomfort.
3. **Add Natural Elements**: Incorporate plants or flowers to bring a touch of nature into your space, promoting tranquility and fresh air.
4. **Soothing Scents and Sounds**: Use essential oils like lavender or chamomile and play soft music or nature sounds to enhance relaxation.
5. **Personal Touch**: Include personal items like a favorite book or a small piece of art that inspires peace and mindfulness.

Mindfulness is all about finding balance amidst the chaos. It's not about eliminating stress entirely but learning to navigate it with grace and ease. So, as you move through your day, try anchoring yourself in the present moment. Notice the details—the way the sunlight dances on the kitchen floor or the sound of rain tapping on the window. These small acts of mindfulness can transform your perspective, bringing peace and balance to your life.

7.3 EMOTIONAL CHECKLISTS: MONITORING YOUR MOOD SWINGS

We've all been there. You're minding your own business, and suddenly, a black cloud hits you. It's like the emotional equivalent of stepping on a LEGO—unexpected and painful. Emotional checklists can be your secret weapon here. Think of them as a mood map that helps you navigate the unpredictable terrain of emotions. Tracking your feelings gives you valuable insights into what sets off those mood swings and how to steer back to calmer waters. It's all about awareness. When you understand what triggers your shifts in mood, you're better equipped to manage them. This isn't just about feeling better—it's about self-regulation and knowing when you might need a little extra self-care or a time-out.

Creating a personalized emotional checklist is like designing your mood's cheat sheet. Start by identifying common emotional triggers and responses. Maybe it's a looming deadline that sends your stress levels soaring or a particular song that always makes you nostalgic. Write these down. Once you've pinpointed the usual suspects, you can craft a simple yet effective checklist format. Keep it straightforward: columns for date, emotion felt, trigger identified, and any actions taken. This isn't a test, so there's no wrong way to do it. The goal is to capture emotions as they come without overthinking or judging them. A checklist can be as simple as a note on your phone or a dedicated page in your planner. Whatever fits seamlessly into your day-to-day life.

Now, here's where it gets interesting. Use these checklists to gain emotional insight. Over time, you'll start to notice patterns.

Maybe you're feeling a bit off every Monday—perhaps the weekend wasn't long enough, or the Monday blues are authentic. By analyzing this data, you can identify patterns and triggers. With this information, you can develop strategies to address those triggers. Perhaps Monday needs a little extra self-care or a morning walk to ease into the week. The checklist becomes a tool for emotional discovery, revealing insights that might otherwise slip by unnoticed. It's like shining a light on the shadowy corners of your emotional landscape, making them less daunting and more manageable.

Integrating emotional checklists into your broader self-care routine is a game-changer. Pairing checklist reviews with activities like journaling or meditation can deepen your insights and enhance your emotional well-being. Imagine starting your day with a quick checklist review and a few minutes of meditation. It's a way to ground yourself and set a positive tone for the day. Or maybe you end your day with a checklist reflection, jotting down any emotional highs and lows you've experienced. This practice not only helps you process your day but also sets the stage for a restful night. Using checklist insights, you can set emotional goals—like aiming for more joy or reducing stress—and track your progress over time. It's about taking small, intentional steps towards a more balanced emotional life.

7.4 BUILDING RESILIENCE: EMBRACING CHANGE WITH STRENGTH

Resilience. It's one of those words that sounds like it belongs in a superhero comic, right next to "invincibility" and "super strength." But unlike those fictional powers, resilience is a real-life skill we can all develop, and there's a good chance you've already started with all the changes in your life going on. It's the ability to bounce back from challenges and face adversity without crumbling. And when you're dealing with the empty nest and all the changes it brings, resilience becomes your trusty sidekick. Psychologists describe resilience as a muscle that strengthens with use. It's not something you're born with; it's something you build over time. History is full of people who have demonstrated incredible resilience. Think of Thomas Edison, who famously said, "I have not failed. I've just found 10,000 ways that won't work," after countless attempts to invent the lightbulb. Edison's story is a testament to the power of perseverance and adaptability—traits that define resilience.

Building resilience involves practical exercises that prepare you for life's curveballs. Scenario planning is one such exercise. It's like a mental fire drill, where you rehearse various outcomes for situations you might face. By envisioning these scenarios, you reduce the shock factor when they occur and feel more equipped to handle them. Cognitive-behavioral strategies are also vital. They help you reframe negative thoughts, turning "I can't do this" into "I can figure this out." It's about challenging those internal narratives that hold you back and replacing them with empowering ones. And while we're at it, let's not forget the importance of physical health. Maintaining a healthy lifestyle supports mental resilience, giving you the energy and clarity to tackle challenges head-on. Regular exercise, a balanced diet, and adequate sleep are the unsung heroes of resilience, keeping your body and mind in peak condition.

Challenges are inevitable, but they're also opportunities for growth and learning. Think of them as life's way of saying, "Here's a chance to learn something new." Many of us have faced adversity and come out stronger on the other side. There's a saying that what doesn't kill you makes you stronger, and there's truth to that. It's like building a callus; each challenge toughens you up a bit more. Personal narratives of overcoming hardship can be incredibly motivating. Take my friend Jake, for example. After losing his job, he saw it not as an end but as a new beginning. He used the setback to pursue his passion for woodworking, eventually turning it into a successful business. Stories like Jake's remind us that setbacks are not failures but stepping stones. To help you reflect on your own experiences, consider prompts like "What did I learn from my last challenge?" or "How did overcoming adversity shape who I am today?"

Cultivating a resilient mindset means embracing change and uncertainty with strength and confidence. It's about looking at the unknown not with fear but with curiosity. One way to foster this mindset is through affirmations and mantras. These are simple phrases that reinforce positive thinking. Try starting your day with an affirmation like, "I am capable of handling whatever comes my way." It's a small practice that can significantly impact your outlook. Developing a personal resilience plan is also valuable. This plan outlines actionable steps for building and maintaining resilience tailored to your needs and goals. Maybe it includes setting aside time each week for self-care or reaching out to a support network when things get tough. Whatever it looks like, your plan should be a living document, adaptable as you grow and change.

By weaving resilience into the fabric of your life, you arm yourself with the tools to face the empty nest transition—and any other challenges—with confidence and grace. Resilience is the foundation for building a fulfilling and adventurous new chapter. The steady ground beneath your feet provides stability as you navigate unfamiliar terrain. As you strengthen your resilience, you'll find that change becomes less daunting and more of an invitation to grow. Embrace this opportunity to evolve, knowing you have the strength to thrive amidst life's unpredictability. With resilience as your ally, you're ready to step into the future with open arms and an open heart.

8

FAITH & FOUNDATIONS: GROUNDING YOURSELF

What do you hold onto when everything you've built your life around changes? For many of us, sending our kids out into the world can leave us feeling uprooted, as though the foundation we relied upon has shifted overnight. The routines, roles, and daily connections that once defined our lives are now different, creating a space we're not quite sure how to fill. This is when we're called to look inward and reconnect with the parts of ourselves that are steady and unchanging.

Grounding ourselves doesn't always mean finding new routines or roles to replace the old ones. Instead, it can mean returning to the core beliefs and values that have been quietly present all along. Faith, in whatever form it takes, provides an anchor—a place to find peace, purpose, and stability amid life's inevitable transitions. When we take the time to pause, reflect, and connect with what gives us strength, the challenges that we face can feel a bit dim.

In its modern context, spirituality is about connecting to something greater than ourselves, whether through nature, meditation, or traditional religious practices. It's about seeking solace and understanding in a chaotic world. Conversely, faith adds a layer of trust and belief, whether in a higher power or in the inherent goodness of life. Together, they provide a sanctuary of peace and resilience. Many folks from our generation, in particular, find spiritual peace as a weekly ritual, with some identifying as religiously unaffiliated yet still deeply connected to their spiritual selves.

So, how do you tap into this wellspring of peace? Spiritual practices can take many forms, each offering its own brand of solace. For some, prayer or contemplation is the key. It's a moment to pause, reflect, and connect with that inner voice often drowned out by the daily grind. Others find reading inspirational texts a balm for the soul, offering wisdom and guidance when the path ahead seems unclear.

Building a supportive spiritual community is another way to ground yourself. Whether through local faith groups or online spiritual forums, these communities offer a shared space to explore and deepen your spiritual practice. Joining a spiritual retreat or workshop can also allow you to step away from life's demands, even just for a weekend, to focus on your spiritual growth. It's like hitting the reset button on your soul. My neighbor, Carol, swears by these retreats, returning with a renewed sense of purpose and a suitcase full of herbal teas she insists are life-changing.

Integrating spirituality into daily life doesn't have to be a grand gesture. It's about weaving moments of reflection and gratitude into the fabric of your day. Morning or evening rituals can set the tone for a day filled with intention and peace. Whether it's a few moments of quiet reflection with your morning coffee or a simple gratitude prayer before bed, these acts serve as gentle reminders of what truly matters. Incorporating service into your routine is another way to live your faith, turning everyday actions into meaningful expressions of spirituality. Helping a neighbor, volunteering, or even just offering a listening ear to a friend can transform the mundane into the sacred.

Interactive Element: Creating Your Spiritual Practice

1. **Daily Check-In**: Set aside five minutes each morning or evening to reflect on your day. What are you grateful for? What challenged you? This brief pause can ground you in gratitude and clarity.
2. **Community Connection**: Join a local or online spiritual group. Attend a meeting or engage in a discussion. Notice how shared experiences enrich your journey.
3. **Inspirational Reading**: Choose a book, poem, or scripture that resonates with you. Spend time each week reading and reflecting on its messages. Consider keeping a journal to capture insights or thoughts that arise.

4. **Acts of Service**: Identify one small act of kindness you can incorporate into your week. Notice how these actions impact your sense of connection and purpose.
5. **Mindful Moment**: Integrate a brief moment of mindfulness into your daily routine. It could be as simple as savoring your morning coffee or taking a few deep breaths before starting your day.

8.1 MEDITATION AND REFLECTION: FINDING INNER CALM

Picture this: you're sitting on your favorite chair, the morning light filtering through the curtains, and there's a moment of stillness where the world pauses. This is where meditation steps in, offering a sanctuary from the chaos. Meditation isn't about sitting cross-legged on a mountain, chanting "Om" (though you can if that's your thing). It's about finding moments of calm amid life's hustle. Many parents, especially those from Generation X, find solace in meditation apps like Headspace or Calm. These apps guide you through the process, offering everything from quick five-minute sessions to longer, more immersive experiences. One popular method is the body scan meditation, which helps you focus on each part of your body, releasing tension you didn't even know you were holding. It's like giving yourself a mini spa day without leaving your living room.

But how do you make meditation a part of your daily life rather than an occasional escape? It's about creating a routine that fits seamlessly into your day. Start by setting aside a specific time—maybe mornings before the house wakes up or evenings when the world quiets down. Consistency is key. Designate a corner of your home as your meditation space. Fill it with calming elements like soft cushions, soothing scents, or gentle music. Think of it as your personal retreat, a place where your mind can wander freely without the demands of daily life. Even a few minutes each day can make a difference, clearing your mental clutter and setting a calm tone for what's ahead.

The benefits of meditation on mental health are backed by science. Studies show regular practice reduces stress and anxiety, improves focus, and enhances emotional regulation. Imagine replacing the constant buzz in your head with a gentle hum of clarity. Meditation helps you respond to stress rather than react, creating a buffer between you and the whirlwind of emotions. It's like having a mental toolkit ready to tackle life's challenges with calm and poise. Over time, you might notice a shift in how you handle everything from morning traffic to that unhelpful email from Karen in accounting.

Reflection and meditation go hand in hand, like peanut butter and jelly. After meditation, take a moment to journal your thoughts. Post-meditation journaling captures insights that bubble up during those quiet moments. It's a space to explore your feelings, jot down realizations, or simply document the random thoughts that pop into your head. Consider asking yourself reflective questions during meditation, such as "What am I grateful for today?" or "What do I need to let go of?" These questions guide your mind toward deeper self-awareness, like a gentle nudge in the right direction. They transform meditation from a passive experience into an active exploration of your inner world.

Interactive Element: Reflective Questions for Meditation

1. What is one thing I appreciate about myself today?
2. What's a small joy I experienced this week?
3. What's causing me stress, and how can I address it with kindness?
4. What's one thing I can forgive myself for?

5. What's a goal I want to focus on, and what small step can I take today?

8.2 SCRIPTURES FOR YOUR JOURNEY

I was raised as a Christian, and those values and verses still pack a strong punch in my heart. Perhaps a practice that might work for you is picking up a Bible each morning and reconnecting with a passage or verse? It's incredible to be able to find such a great amount of clarity and solace in just a few minutes a day. The bonus here is that there are so many passages that can resonate with us as empty nest Christians.

Isaiah 46:4: *"Even to your old age I am he, and to gray hairs I will carry you. I have made, and I will bear; I will carry and will save."*

This verse is a beautiful reminder that, even as life transitions and our children grow independent, God is a constant source of support, guidance, and strength. It speaks to the assurance that we are not alone in this new chapter and that God continues to carry and sustain us, just as we have cared for our children.

Another encouraging verse is **Proverbs 22:6**: *"Train up a child in the way he should go; even when he is old, he will not depart from it."*

I love this one. Here, King Solomon highlights the comfort that comes from knowing you've laid a foundation of values and faith for your children. Even as they venture out independently, your shared teachings and love will continue to guide them.

Consider **Jeremiah 29:11:** *"For I know the plans I have for you, declares the Lord, plans for welfare and not for evil, to give you a future and a hope."*

Could this work for both you and your children? Of course. As your kids enter adulthood, you can trust that God has a plan for them and for you, a plan that brings hope and purpose in every season of life.

I would be remiss not to mention the verse of all verses, **John 3:16-17:** *"For God so loved the world, that he gave his only Son, that whoever believes in him should not perish but have eternal life. For God did not send his Son into the world to condemn the world, but in order that the world might be saved through him."*

In his own celestial way, God experienced an empty nest of sorts when Jesus left the heavens to come to Earth and make the ultimate sacrifice for humanity. Imagine the profound love it required for God to send His only Son away, knowing the challenges, pain, and eventual suffering that awaited him. Just as earthly parents release their children to follow their own paths, God released Jesus to fulfill a divine purpose that would bring salvation and hope to all. This act was a testament to the depth of God's love for us—a willingness to let go for a greater good, trusting in the ultimate plan even as the heavens felt his absence. In this way, God's own experience of "empty nest" reflects a love that is sacrificial, enduring, and overflowing with grace.

As you step into this new phase, finding comfort and guidance in scripture can provide a strong foundation for your journey. Bible verses offer timeless wisdom on purpose, change, and trusting in God's plan—especially in moments when the quiet house feels overwhelming or you're questioning your next steps. **Jeremiah 29:11** says, *"For I know the plans I have for you,"* declares the Lord, *"plans to prosper you and not to harm you, plans to give you hope and a future."* In times of transition, this verse is a powerful reminder that God's vision for us goes beyond our roles as parents. It reassures us that there is a unique purpose in every stage of life, even as our roles shift.

8.3 SPIRITUAL PRACTICES: FAITH AS YOUR ANCHOR

I've always liked the metaphor of faith like a ship anchored in a safe harbor. Spiritual practices can be that anchor, providing comfort and guidance when life feels like a swirling sea. Many find solace in daily prayer and devotionals, those quiet moments where you connect with the divine or simply reflect on life's mysteries over a cup of tea. It's about creating a dialogue with something bigger than yourself, whether that's God, the universe, or the wisdom of your own heart. This daily ritual can be as simple as whispering a few words of gratitude or spending a few minutes in silent reverie, aligning your spirit with the day ahead.

Rituals from different faith traditions offer inspiration and grounding. Consider lighting a candle to symbolize clarity or setting intentions with incense smoke wafting through the air. These rituals connect us to centuries of tradition, reminding us we're part of a larger tapestry of belief and history. Whether it's the calming rhythm of a rosary, the serene mindfulness of a Zen tea ceremony, or the vibrant energy of a Hindu aarti, these practices infuse our lives with meaning. They're like spiritual pit stops, moments to refuel and recalibrate amidst the chaos. My friend, Julie, finds inspiration in her Sunday ritual of reading psalms, a practice that brings peace and reflection to her week.

Integrating faith into daily life doesn't require grand gestures. It's about weaving spirituality into the fabric of your everyday routine. Morning or evening prayers can bookend your day, offering a moment to reflect on what you're grateful for or seeking guidance for the challenges ahead. Reading spiritual texts or scriptures regularly keeps you connected to your beliefs and provides a wellspring of wisdom. These readings gently remind you of the principles you hold dear, like a lighthouse guiding your path. Think of it as having a conversation with the sages of old, who've faced life's trials and emerged wiser.

Community plays a vital role in strengthening faith and encouraging spiritual growth. Joining faith-based groups or congregations provides a sense of belonging and shared purpose. It's about connecting with others who walk a similar path, sharing experiences, and supporting one another in times of doubt or celebration. Participating in faith-led volunteer work or missions extends this connection beyond the spiritual, turning beliefs into actions that impact the wider world. Whether you're serving meals at a local shelter or building homes in a far-off land, these acts of service embody the principles of your faith, offering tangible expressions of love and compassion.

Navigating life's challenges with faith as your compass can be profoundly comforting. Spiritual teachings often provide a framework for understanding and overcoming adversity, like a map guiding you through uncharted territory. Turning to these teachings can offer solace and strength during difficult times, reminding you that you're not alone. Faith-based support systems, such as prayer circles or study groups, encourage resilience, offering a space to share burdens and joys. These communities become sanctuaries where the collective strength of shared belief uplifts and sustains.

8.4 GRATITUDE JOURNALS: CULTIVATING THANKFULNESS

Gratitude, it turns out, is more than just a feel-good buzzword. It's a practice that can lead to increased happiness and improved well-being. Studies show that people who regularly engage in gratitude exercises tend to be happier and less stressed. It's like adding a splash of sunshine to your mental landscape, brightening even the gloomiest days. And it's not just about you—

gratitude can transform relationships, too. A simple "thank you" can strengthen bonds, making connections feel more profound and more genuine. Imagine the ripple effect of appreciation spreading through your circle, creating waves of positivity.

Now, let's talk about starting a gratitude journaling routine. Think of it as your personal treasure chest, where you stash moments of joy and appreciation. You don't need a fancy notebook or a calligraphy pen; a simple journal will do. Begin with daily or weekly entries, jotting down three things you're grateful for. They can be as grand as a promotion at work or as simple as a stranger's smile. If you ever feel stuck, prompts can help guide your reflections. Consider questions like, "Who made me smile today?" or "What am I looking forward to?" These prompts act as gentle nudges, encouraging you to notice the good things that often go overlooked. As you fill your journal, you'll create a collection of positivity, a reminder of the beauty in everyday life.

But gratitude doesn't have to stay confined to the pages of a journal. It can be woven into your daily interactions and spiritual practices. Expressing gratitude verbally to loved ones can strengthen connections and create an atmosphere of warmth and appreciation. Imagine the impact of telling a friend, "I really appreciate how you always listen to me," or thanking a colleague for their support. These small acts of kindness ripple outward, fostering a culture of gratitude. Expressing thankfulness to the Creator in prayer or contemplation can solidify those moments we take for granted. Consider incorporating acts of kindness into your routine as expressions of gratitude. Holding the door for someone, writing a heartfelt note, or surprising a friend with their favorite treat can be powerful ways to say "thank you" without words.

Reflecting on gratitude over time can reveal patterns and growth you might not have noticed. Review past journal entries to see how your perspective has shifted. Maybe you've become more aware of the little joys in life, or perhaps you've noticed a newfound appreciation for certain people or experiences. Creating a gratitude timeline can help visualize these changes. Highlight significant events or moments that stand out, mapping your journey from where you began to where you are now. This timeline becomes a testament to your growth, a visual reminder of how gratitude has enriched your life. As you look back, you'll see how each entry, each expression of thanks, has shaped your outlook and brought you closer in your spiritual life.

8.5 PURPOSEFUL LIVING: ALIGNING ACTIONS WITH VALUES

It's time to put this chapter into practice. The values and standards that you've defined act as your personal compass, steering your decisions and actions. Think about the moments when you felt truly at peace or, conversely, when something felt off. These instances often reveal what matters most to you. Consider engaging in values assessment exercises to help pinpoint these guiding principles. Reflect on past decisions, both good and bad, to uncover patterns that reveal your true priorities. This reflection is like a treasure hunt, unearthing the truths that lie beneath the surface.

Once you've identified your core values, the next step is ensuring your daily actions support them. This is where a personal mission statement comes into play. Crafting one can seem daunting, but it's simply a declaration of what you stand for and hope to achieve. It serves as a touchstone, a reminder of your purpose when life gets hectic. Setting daily intentions that align with these values is another powerful practice. It's like setting the GPS for your day, ensuring that each action moves you closer to your ultimate destination. These intentions don't have to be grand; they can be as simple as choosing kindness in a difficult situation or dedicating time to a passion project.

Living with intentionality means approaching each day with purpose and mindfulness. It's about making choices that reflect your values rather than reacting to circumstances. Mindful decision-making practices can help you navigate life's challenges with clarity. Before deciding, pause and ask yourself: Does this align with my values? Will this choice bring me closer to the life I want to live? Regular reflection on your life alignment with values helps keep you on track, allowing you to course-correct when needed. It's like a regular tune-up for your soul, ensuring you run smoothly and efficiently.

Life is full of changes, and as an empty nest parent, viewing these transitions through the lens of both your values and your faith can provide guidance and a sense of peace. In this new chapter, decision-making grounded in spiritual principles can help light your path, whether you're contemplating a new career direction, considering a move, or navigating shifts in relationships. Reflecting on these choices with God's wisdom as your foundation brings a calm assurance, reminding you that you are supported even as life takes unexpected turns.

Setting values-based and faith-centered goals, both personally and professionally, can be especially meaningful in this season. When your goals are rooted in what truly matters to you—and are aligned with your faith—they bring a sense of fulfillment that goes beyond simply "staying busy." This alignment turns your dreams into purposeful steps, creating a roadmap that resonates with your true self and God's intentions for you.

You'll find a growing harmony between your actions, values, and faith as you bring these practices into your daily life. This alignment doesn't happen overnight, especially with the many changes that come with an empty nest, but through prayer, patience, and reflection, a newfound sense of clarity and direction emerges. Along this journey, God walks with you, providing reassurance and strength, making the path as fulfilling as the destination.

Living purposefully makes each journey step worthwhile, filling your days with intention, clarity, and spiritual grounding. You open yourself to a life of depth and meaning by aligning your actions with your values and faith. With this foundation, you're prepared for the next chapter, where we'll explore how to face life's inevitable ups and downs with resilience, grace, and the steady guidance of your faith.

9

"I'M BACK, JUST KIDDING!" NOW WHAT?

Remember the day you first sent your kids off to college with a mix of pride and a lump in your throat? You've finally moved past the initial shock and adjusted to life in a quieter home. Recall my son's room of baseball trophies? For a while, it sat as a shrine to their teenage years, complete with posters and bobbleheads. Maybe by now you transformed that old room into a gym or a home office. You've even found ways to fill your free time—you don't remember your social calendar being this busy! You've made inspiring and important strides to acceptance.

Then, one Sunday afternoon, you get a phone call from your adult child expressing a desire to return home. Soon. For a long-term visit. Suddenly, you're back to stocking up on their favorite snacks and hearing the familiar sound of their footsteps echoing in the hallway. Welcome to the world of boomerang kids, a phenomenon as common now as selfies and avocado toast. How are we going to figure this one out?

9.1 BACK TO THE NEST: STRATEGIES FOR SUCCESS

The trend of adult children returning home is surging, fueled by economic challenges that would make anyone's head spin. According to Thrivent's 2024 Boomerang Kids Survey, nearly half of parents have welcomed their adult offspring back home, primarily due to skyrocketing housing costs. Young adults are grappling with rising rents, which have become a formidable foe, forcing them to retreat to the safety of their childhood bedrooms. And let's not forget the mountain of student debt looming over them like a financial Everest. Many young adults delay significant milestones like buying a home or saving for retirement as they juggle student loans and meager paychecks. It's no wonder they find solace in the familiar refuge of home, where the rent is, potentially, free.

As your child hauls in their belongings and reclaims their old room (or your new gym), it's crucial to establish household rules that keep everyone sane. Think of it as creating a playbook for this new chapter. Clear rules and expectations are the backbone of a harmonious household. Shared responsibilities, like chores and managing finances, must be outlined from the start. Maybe it's time for your child to perfect their vacuuming skills or finally tackle those dishes without being asked. It's also important to address privacy and space. Remember, your child is no longer a teenager, and they need their own space just as much as you do. Consider setting boundaries around communal areas and respecting each other's need for solitude.

Fostering independence while living under the same roof can feel like walking a tightrope—but it's doable. Encourage your child to contribute financially to household expenses, even if it's a small amount. This not only eases the financial burden on you but also instills a sense of responsibility in them. While you certainly need to keep the gas out of your helicopter, you're still there to guide and inspire like you always have. Support their educational or career goals by providing a stable environment where they can focus on growth. Whether studying for exams or navigating job applications, your home should be a springboard for their ambitions, not a comfy couch to crash on indefinitely. It's about striking a balance between being supportive and fostering self-sufficiency.

Navigating the emotional dynamics of living with adult children requires finesse, patience, and a dash of humor. It's normal for tensions to arise as both parties adjust to this new arrangement. Open communication is your ally here. Create an atmosphere where everyone feels comfortable expressing concerns or frustrations. Regular family meetings can be a great way to clear the air and realign expectations. Approach these discussions with empathy, acknowledging the stress and pressure your child might be experiencing. Supporting their mental health is paramount, as the transition back home can be challenging. Encourage them to seek professional support if needed and be there to offer a listening ear and a comforting presence.

Exercise: Crafting Your Household Rules

1. **List Your Priorities**: Identify what matters most to you in maintaining a harmonious household. Is it cleanliness, privacy, or financial contributions? Write down your top 3 priorities.
2. **Discuss with Your Child**: Have an open conversation about these priorities. Ask for their input and listen to their concerns. This collaborative approach helps foster mutual respect.
3. **Set Financial Expectations**: If feasible, agree on a reasonable financial contribution from your child so they have some "skin in the game." This could be a small rent or a portion of utilities. Discuss payment methods and deadlines.
4. **Establish a Weekly Check-In**: Schedule a weekly meeting to discuss issues, celebrate successes, and adjust rules as needed. Use this time to connect and strengthen your relationship.

9.2 SETTING BOUNDARIES: ENCOURAGING HEALTHY INDEPENDENCE

So, your adult child is back home, and suddenly, the lines between parent and roommate begin to blur. It's a delicate dance, navigating the new dynamics without stepping on each other's toes. This is where setting healthy boundaries comes into play. But what exactly are healthy boundaries in an adult parent-child relationship? Think of them as the guidelines that help maintain mutual respect and independence. They aren't rigid walls that isolate or are so flimsy that they collapse at the slightest pressure. Healthy boundaries are like well-tended garden fences; they protect and define spaces without obstructing the view.

Boundaries that are too rigid can stifle growth, leading to resentment and tension. It's like living in a house with locked doors you can't open. On the flip side, too lax boundaries might leave you feeling overwhelmed or taken for granted, as if your home has no walls at all. Finding the sweet spot is key. For instance, establishing a boundary where your child knows to call if they're going to be late respects both your peace of mind and their autonomy. Or, agreeing on certain chores ensures that the household runs smoothly without anyone feeling like they're bearing the brunt of the work.

Respecting your child's autonomy is pivotal in nurturing their growth. Remember, they're adults now, and while they may be living under your roof, they still need room to make their own decisions. That means resisting the urge to offer unsolicited advice or micromanage their choices. Encourage them to solve problems independently, even if that means biting your tongue when you see them heading down a path you wouldn't have chosen. Supporting their decision-making process, rather than dictating it, empowers them to develop confidence and resilience. It's like teaching them to ride a bike all over again—eventually, you have to let go of the seat.

As life unfolds, boundaries may need to evolve. Relationships are dynamic, and what works today might not be suitable tomorrow. Regular check-ins can help reassess these boundaries and ensure they continue to serve everyone involved. These check-ins are maintenance checks for your relationship, ensuring everything runs smoothly. Flexibility is key, allowing room for adjustments as circumstances change. Whether it's a new job, a budding relationship, or simply a change in perspective, being open to renegotiating boundaries keeps the relationship healthy and vibrant.

9.3 OPPORTUNITIES FOR GROWTH

When Jane's daughter Sandy left for college, Jane thought she'd finally entered the empty nest stage for good. Sandy was independent, thriving in her career and building a life in another city. But then, life threw a curveball, as it so often does. Sandy's company downsized, leaving her without a job, and her lease was up shortly after. Before Jane knew it, Sandy was back at home, lugging boxes through the front door as they both tried to navigate the reality of her return.

Having her back was both comforting and surreal for Jane. Once adapted to an empty, quiet home, her daily rhythms had to shift and accommodate a new dynamic. She had her own routines and ways of doing things, and Jane had to remind herself that she wasn't the same teenager she had watched leave years ago. Jane quickly realized that what had felt like her space was now their shared space again.

They had to navigate simple things—who got to use the kitchen first in the morning, who was doing laundry, and when. But it was the larger, unspoken adjustments that took them both by surprise. Slowly, they fell into a rhythm. Jane learned to give Sandy space to figure things out independently, resisting the urge to parent her as she used to. And Sandy found ways to contribute, helping around the house and making dinner a few nights a week. Living together again was a balancing act, but it also allowed them to reconnect more deeply. There was no doubt that there were challenges, but so was a new sense of understanding and respect for each other as adults.

When your child moves back in, it can feel like pressing the rewind button on your family life. But this can be a golden opportunity to strengthen relationships and rediscover connections with your adult children, far beyond what you experienced when they were younger. It's like getting to know a new person who just happens to have your family's nose. Adult children bring new perspectives shaped by their experiences outside the home. These are the same kids who, not too long ago, needed help with their homework and now might be able to teach you a thing or two about the latest tech trend or social issue. This time together can be a rich ground for conversations and a chance to understand their world and share yours. It's like opening a book with new chapters that you both can explore.

Rediscovering this connection involves peeling back layers that might have formed over years of rushed dinners and teenage angst. It's about finding common ground and allowing conversations to blossom naturally. Maybe you bond over shared interests, like a love for cooking or a passion for politics. Perhaps you discover new ones, like a mutual appreciation for a TV series or a sport. These shared interests become the glue that strengthens your relationship, providing touchpoints that keep you connected even when life gets busy.

Creating new family traditions can be an unexpected delight in this arrangement. Imagine Friday nights becoming dedicated family game nights or Sunday afternoons reserved for a family hike or a trip to the farmer's market. These traditions don't have to be elaborate; they just need to be consistent. They create a sense of rhythm and anticipation for everyone to look forward to amidst the week's chaos. It's about carving out a space for togetherness, where laughter and camaraderie are the main ingredients. These shared experiences can turn ordinary moments into cherished memories, strengthening the familial bond in ways you never thought possible.

In this shared living situation, the key is to approach each day with openness and a willingness to learn from one another. Your child's return is not just about the challenges of cohabiting but also about the growth opportunities it presents. It's a chance to see each other as parents and children and individuals with unique stories and strengths. Embrace the changes, savor the shared moments, and view this phase as a chapter of growth and connection, an unexpected yet rewarding twist in the ongoing narrative of your family.

9.4 THE SILVER LINING

It's a funny thing, really—finding joy in chaos. But that's exactly what happens when your adult child returns home. You might have thought the days of stepping over their laundry or hearing their music blaring from the next room were over. Yet, here they are, back with all their quirks, and somehow, it's endearing. There's a certain charm in the unexpected moments that unfold. Like when you catch them raiding the fridge at midnight, just like old times, or when you find yourselves laughing uncontrollably over a silly TV show you both secretly love. These little slices of life remind us that there's beauty to be found even amid chaos. It's about embracing these moments, allowing them to warm your heart, and realizing that the noise and clutter are not just distractions but signs of life—vibrant, messy, wonderful life.

Living under one roof again offers a chance to experience the benefits of multi-generational living, a trend gaining traction as families come together for various reasons. There's something deeply comforting about having multiple generations living side by side. It creates a wealth of experiences where stories from the past mingle with dreams for the future. The shared responsibilities can lighten the load for everyone involved. Maybe you find yourself in the kitchen, cooking a meal while your child sets the table, and suddenly, the task feels less like a chore and more like a shared ritual. Emotional support becomes a two-way street where you offer wisdom and guidance. In return, you receive fresh perspectives and companionship. It's a dynamic that breaks the isolation often felt in single-generation households, replacing it with a sense of belonging and shared purpose.

This living arrangement also brings financial benefits, as it can ease the burden of housing costs for both generations. Shared expenses make homeownership more affordable, allowing everyone to save for other goals or simply enjoy more financial breathing room. It's about pooling resources and creating a stronger collective than its individual parts. And beyond the practical, there's the emotional richness that comes from living together. You're not just sharing a space; you're sharing lives, weaving together memories and experiences that become the fabric of your family's story. The laughter, the shared meals, the quiet evenings spent together—they all contribute to a deeper understanding and appreciation of one another.

It's important, however, to remember that this time together is not just a pause in their journey; it's a launching pad for what comes next. Your home is where they can regroup, gather strength, and prepare for their next steps. It's a safety net that allows them to explore options without the overwhelming pressure of immediate financial independence. As they plan their future, you have the opportunity to be a sounding board, offering advice and encouragement as they outline their goals and dreams. In this way, your home becomes a springboard, propelling them into a future filled with potential and promise.

As this chapter closes, think of the possibilities that lie ahead—both for you and your child. This time together is a gift, a chance to reconnect, learn, and grow. Embrace the chaos, savor the moments, and look to the future with hope and excitement. As you move into the next chapter, carry the lessons learned and bonds strengthened, ready to face whatever comes next with an open heart and a sense of adventure.

10

BEYOND THE NEST: EMBRACING THE JOYFUL UNKNOWN

When Brian's son Jacob told him he was quitting his stable job to become a traveling musician, Brian panicked a little. After years of helping him find his footing, seeing him walk away from stability was tough. But he had that determined look, the one that told Dad he'd already made up his mind. So, Brian bit his tongue and tried to support him as best as he could, even though he worried about the uncertain path ahead.

There were challenging moments, like the night Jacob called, ready to quit after his band's equipment broke down. Every instinct told Brian to say, "Come home, Jacob." Instead, he encouraged him to keep going, reminding him of the resilience Dad had seen in him over the years. Supporting him through this journey, even with all its risks, became an unexpected lesson in trust—for both of them.

Over time, Brian saw Jacob grow in ways he hadn't anticipated. He became more resilient, learned patience, and discovered what living with an open heart meant. His choice taught Brian that sometimes the best way to support our children is by letting them follow their own path, trusting they'll find their way—and knowing we'll be there no matter what.

Maintaining a solid relationship with your children as they navigate their adult lives requires a foundation built on respect. This isn't just about nodding politely when they mention their latest tattoo or that new diet they're trying. It's about recognizing and valuing their perspectives, even when they differ from your own. Remember, they've inherited a bit of your stubborn streak, so it's no surprise they might have strong opinions. Avoiding judgment or criticism of their life choices is crucial. Sure, you might have raised an eyebrow when they decided to backpack through Europe with nothing but a ukulele, but their journeys are shaping who they are. Your role now is to be a supportive figure who appreciates their individuality, offering guidance only when asked.

Distance can complicate maintaining close family ties, but it's entirely possible with a bit of creativity. Regularly scheduled calls or video chats are a godsend, offering a lifeline to stay connected. Technology, once the bane of family dinners, is now your ally. Set up weekly video calls where everyone can catch up, share stories, and perhaps even play a virtual game or two. And why not get a little creative with it? Start a family newsletter, a digital keepsake where each member can contribute updates, photos, and even a little humor. It's like your very own family magazine, chronicling achievements and milestones. This keeps everyone in the loop and strengthens the bond across miles.

Even as you maintain a close connection, respecting privacy and space is paramount. Your kids are carving out their identities and need room to grow. Understanding boundaries around personal information is essential. Instead of grilling them on every detail of their lives, give them the freedom to share their choices. It's about balancing involvement with independence, allowing them to come to you when they're ready. Just because you chat regularly doesn't mean you need to know every detail of their daily life. Trust that they'll share the important stuff and, in the meantime, show interest in their passions and pursuits without prying.

Celebrating individual achievements is a wonderful way to reinforce mutual respect and appreciation. When your child lands that dream job or completes a challenging project, acknowledge it with a personalized congratulatory message. Maybe it's a handwritten note, a digital card, or even a small gift that shows you're thinking of them. Planning visits around significant achievements can also be substantial. Whether attending their graduation ceremony or simply being there when they receive an award, these moments create lasting memories emphasizing your support and pride in their accomplishments.

10.1 SUPPORTING ADULT CHILDREN'S LIFE CHOICES

You can imagine standing at a crossroads with your child, each path leading to a different future. They're ready to choose, and your role now is to be the wise old sage, not the traffic cop. Providing unconditional support for your adult children's life choices is a bit like being their personal cheerleader but without the pom-poms. It's about standing by them as they explore diverse paths, whether it's a sudden career change or an unexpected lifestyle choice. Maybe they've decided to pursue a career in organic farming after years of studying accounting. It's a twist worthy of a sitcom, but it's their twist. Your task is to support their decision without judgment, understanding that their journey may look nothing like what you imagined. Resist the urge to compare them to their peers or siblings. Each person's path is unique, and the comparisons only serve to undermine their confidence.

Being a source of guidance is more about listening than directing. Think of it as guiding your children down a path lit by their ambitions, not your expectations. Share your experiences, but do it without imposing your outcomes. Your stories are a treasure trove of wisdom, but they're not blueprints for your child's life. Encourage them to explore and discover what fulfills them, even if it means they might stumble a bit along the way. The beauty of self-discovery is in the journey itself, with all its bumps and turns. Offer insights that empower rather than dictate. Instead of saying, "You should do this," try, "Have you considered this option?" It's a subtle shift that leaves room for their own decision-making.

Respecting their decisions and outcomes is crucial, even when things don't go according to plan. Your child might decide to backpack across South America in search of inspiration, only to come back with a suitcase full of stories and a few new skills. Practicing acceptance and non-judgment allows them to learn from their experiences without the fear of disappointing you. When they make a decision that doesn't pan out as expected, offer help when they ask for it, not before. It's important they know you're there, ready to support them, but without overshadowing their autonomy. Let them come to you when they're ready, knowing you'll be there with open arms and a smile.

Fostering open dialogue about life choices is the glue that holds your relationship together. It's about creating a space where they feel safe to share their dreams, fears, and everything in between. Use active listening techniques to show you're genuinely interested in what they have to say. Rephrase their words to confirm understanding, and ask open-ended questions to keep the conversation flowing. This isn't an interrogation; it's a dance of communication where both parties feel heard and valued. Make it a point to have these discussions in a relaxed setting, perhaps over a casual dinner or a walk in the park. The goal is to make it feel less like a board meeting and more like a heart-to-heart chat.

In these conversations, avoiding the pitfalls of offering unsolicited advice is important. Instead, focus on understanding their perspective. Ask questions encouraging them to reflect on their choices, such as, "What excites you most about this path?" This allows them to articulate their motivations and gain clarity while you gain insight into their thought process. It's about building a bridge of understanding that connects your world with theirs, fostering a relationship rooted in trust and mutual respect. Through these dialogues, you become not just a parent but a trusted confidant who's there to support their journey, wherever it may lead.

10.2 THE FUTURE OF FAMILY GATHERINGS: CELEBRATING MILESTONES

Planning inclusive family events is a bit like orchestrating a symphony, where each family member, regardless of age or stage of life, plays a unique part in the melody. You might find joy in creating gatherings that bring together everyone's interests, bridging the gap between generations and making space for each person's place in the family. It's about ensuring Uncle Joe can enjoy the bocce ball game just as much as your teenage niece loves the karaoke setup in the corner. Now, with a quiet home most of the time, these gatherings become moments to reconnect and cherish, allowing you to see how your family has grown, changed, and diversified. Activities that engage all age groups—like board games for the strategists, a painting station for the artists, and a storytelling corner where grandparents can share family lore—allow you to witness the family's collective journey.

Family milestones, such as a grandchild's graduation or your own wedding anniversary, take on an even more profound significance in the empty nest years. These are life's punctuation marks, the milestones that unite the family and underscore the importance of each individual's story within the family's legacy. Hosting these celebrations might seem overwhelming, but they can strengthen bonds and create lasting memories. Building a family photo album, for instance, allows you to capture these cherished moments—a chance to document the love and laughter that fill your home when it's bustling with family once again.

Balancing tradition and innovation in family gatherings becomes a rewarding dance, especially when you can pass down beloved traditions while making space for new ideas. Perhaps there's a long-standing summer potluck tradition in your family. Adding a modern touch—like a digital slideshow of family memories or a video booth where everyone can leave messages for future generations—invites younger family members to shape their roles in these gatherings. Watching them breathe new life into old customs keeps family gatherings vibrant. It allows you to see your family legacy evolve through their eyes.

Navigating family dynamics as an empty nester requires diplomacy and a sense of humor, especially when conversations drift into sensitive topics. Open communication and ground rules can go a long way in ensuring that gatherings remain harmonious. Remind everyone that these moments celebrate togetherness and a time to embrace shared values and memories. For an empty nest parent, gatherings like these are about more than just the event itself—they're about creating an inclusive, meaningful space where each family member feels connected and valued. These moments become treasured chapters in your family's story, weaving together threads of past and present, laughter and love, reminding you of the beautiful blended mess that is your family.

10.3 PREPARING FOR GRANDPARENTHOOD

Becoming a grandparent is like being handed a golden ticket to a new adventure. Maybe you remember your own grandparents and how they seemed to have the answers to life's biggest questions, all while sneaking you extra cookies when your parents weren't looking. Now, it's your turn to decide what kind of grandparent you want to be. This is more than just a title; it's an opportunity to set intentions for the relationship you'll build with your grandchildren. Will you be the storyteller, the confidant, the adventurer? Each visit is a chance to create memories that will last a lifetime, so think about what you want those memories to look like.

As you're buckling your grandchild into the huge UFO-like child seat in your car, you might recall your parents not even having seat belts in the family car! Times change, and as you step into this role, it's important to balance your involvement in your grandchildren's lives with respecting parental boundaries. Let's face it, parenting styles have changed since you were a new parent! Your adult children may have different ideas about raising their kids, too, and that's okay. Understanding their preferences and limits is vital to maintaining a harmonious relationship. It might be tempting to offer advice on everything from bedtime routines to the best way to soothe a crying baby, but sometimes, the best support is simply being there without overstepping. Offer your wisdom when asked, and remember that your role is to enhance their parenting experience, not override it.

Building solid relationships with your grandchildren is a beautiful endeavor that requires intention and creativity. Plan regular visits and activities that allow you to bond without the distractions of everyday life. Maybe it's a monthly sleepover at Grandma and Grandpa's house, complete with popcorn and movies. Or perhaps it's a Saturday morning tradition of pancake breakfasts followed by a trip to the park. Creating traditions or rituals unique to your grandparent-grandchild bond can be incredibly meaningful. These shared experiences become the stories your grandchildren will tell about you someday.

Supporting your adult children as they navigate their roles as parents is another crucial aspect of grandparenthood. Remember the chaos and uncertainty you felt as a new parent? Now's your chance to offer a helping hand, providing practical support like childcare or the occasional home-cooked meal. This support can be a lifeline during their busiest days. However, offering advice when asked without imposing your own parenting philosophies is important. Every family needs to find its own rhythm, and your role is to be a steady presence, offering guidance when sought and a listening ear when needed.

Grandparenthood is undoubtedly a joyful chapter, but it also comes with its own set of challenges. As your family grows, you may find yourself juggling the demands of multiple generations. It's a balancing act that requires patience, understanding, and a touch of humor. After all, nothing says you're a grandparent quite like discovering a toddler's toy wedged in your couch cushions or finding a crayon masterpiece on your freshly painted walls. Embrace these moments with a smile, knowing that the love you share with your grandchildren is worth every bit of the occasional chaos.

The transition into grandparenthood is a journey of growth, love, and discovery. Each moment spent with your grandchildren is a chance to impart wisdom, share laughter, and create memories that will endure. As you look forward to this new chapter, embrace the opportunity to be a guiding light in your family's life, just as your own grandparents were for you. So, whether you're planning the next big family gathering or enjoying a quiet afternoon with your grandchild, cherish these moments. Soak in the feels when you hear the same chuckle from little Timmy that your son made years ago. Find the humor in the situation when little Alice chucks broccoli across the room like your daughter used to. You'll have to return them home eventually, and guess what? That just gives you an excuse to see a particular grown kid you love.

CONCLUSION

As you reach the end of this book, I hope you've found encouragement, insights, and a renewed sense of purpose for this chapter of your life. The empty nest isn't a place of endings; it's a place of beginnings—a time to rediscover who you are, redefine the values that matter most, and reimagine your relationship with yourself, your family, and the world around you. We've laughed, probably cried a little, and certainly shared a few "aha" moments along the way. From the initial shock of finding yourself with a newfound silence to the thrilling opportunity to reinvent and rediscover yourself, this journey has been nothing short of transformative.

Remember our chat about reinventing your identity? That moment of staring in the mirror and asking, "Who even am I now?" Well, I hope you've found a few answers—or at least started asking the right questions. Whether you've dusted off an old hobby or embarked on a new adventure, the key takeaway is that this phase of life is as much about you as it is about them.

So, what should you carry forward from all this? First, embrace the idea that this transition is a golden opportunity for growth.

You have the chance to explore passions you put on hold, to nurture relationships that took a backseat, and to cultivate new ones that bring joy and fulfillment. We've armed you with practical strategies—from journaling to meditation, from setting boundaries to embracing new social dynamics—to help guide you through this new landscape.

But, as we've said, the magic happens when you take those small, consistent steps. Start with something simple: a new hobby, a commitment to a weekly date night, or maybe a volunteer project that speaks to your heart. These aren't just actions; they're seeds. And with a little nurturing, they'll grow into something beautiful.

And now, here's my call to action for you. Stand tall, embrace this chapter with open arms, and dive into the life waiting for you beyond the nest. The strategies and tools we've discussed are yours for the taking, ready to transform your everyday into an extraordinary shelf of experiences. Trust in your ability to create a life full of purpose and joy.

I also want to remind you that you're not alone. As a parent who's been through it all—I get it. I've felt the same pangs of loss and the same bursts of liberation. This book is here to be a companion, a trusty sidekick as you navigate these waters. So when you hit a snag, flip back through these pages. Find that advice, that exercise, that story that resonates with you, and lean on it.

Before I let you go, I want to extend a heartfelt thank you for allowing me to be part of your journey. It's been an honor to share this time with you, to swap stories, and to cheer you on from the sidelines. Remember, this isn't just a book; it's a community—a space where we all support and uplift each other through the ups and downs of the empty nest.

So here's to you, my fellow adventurer. May your days be filled with new discoveries, your heart with endless gratitude, and your spirit with boundless enthusiasm. You've got this. And if ever you need a reminder, just flip back to these pages. I'm cheering for you every step of the way.

REFERENCES

The Empty Nest Has Benefits (and Challenges) for Parents https://www.psychologytoday.com/us/blog/the-right-side-of-40/202306/the-empty-nest-has-benefits-and-challenges-for-parents

The Benefits of Solitude and How to Get the Most from Your ... https://tinybuddha.com/blog/the-benefits-of-solitude-and-how-to-get-the-most-from-your-alone-time/

Have adult kids? Here's how to support without overstepping. https://extramile.thehartford.com/family/parenting/supporting-adult-children/

How to Transition from Parent to Mentor: Building a Strong ... https://medium.com/@drmattkutz/how-to-transition-from-parent-to-mentor-building-a-strong-relationship-with-your-adult-kids-f44c1ce011cb

Finding Identity and Overcoming the Empty Nest https://firststepsrecovery.com/finding-identity-and-overcoming-the-empty-nest/

Empty Nest Syndrome https://www.psychologytoday.com/us/conditions/empty-nest-syndrome

21 Best Tips for Reinventing Yourself After Empty Nest https://www.the-trybe.com/post/reinventing-yourself-after-empty-nest

Inspiring professionals who prove a midlife career change ... https://www.umassglobal.edu/news-and-events/blog/inspiring-professionals-who-prove-a-midlife-career-change-is-possible

How Social Connection Supports Longevity https://longevity.stanford.edu/lifestyle/2023/12/18/how-social-connection-supports-longevity/

Find a Volunteer Opportunity Near You https://www.unitedway.org/get-involved/volunteer

Balance between solitude and socializing: everyday ... https://www.ncbi.nlm.nih.gov/pmc/articles/PMC10698034/

The Empty Nest Syndrome - The Gen X Journey Podcast https://podcasts.apple.com/us/podcast/the-empty-nest-syndrome/id1660961159?i=1000669316039

The Myth of the Empty Nest - Southbay https://www.oursouthbay.com/the-myth-of-the-empty-nest/

Rekindling a Marriage As Empty Nesters https://www.focusonthefamily.com/family-qa/rekindling-a-marriage-as-empty-nesters/

Schnelle, A. (n.d.). Volunteer Opportunities are Out There. Holy Family Lamp Post. https://hflamppost.com/1431/features/volunteer-opportunities-are-out-there/https://hflamppost.com/1431/features/volunteer-opportunities-are-out-there/

REKINDLING YOUR RELATIONSHIP IN THE EMPTY NESThttps://www.crestingthehill.com.au/2016/08/reconnecting-in-empty-nest.html

Empty Nest Syndrome In Marriage And How Couples Can Cope https://www.sdrelationshipplace.com/empty-nest-syndrome-in-marriage/

How I Overcame My Loneliness As A Single Mom https://www.rootsofloneliness.com/single-mom-loneliness

10 Budgeting Tips for Single Parents https://www.incharge.org/financial-literacy/budgeting-saving/single-parents/

A Single Parent's Path to Community https://www.focusonthefamily.com/parenting/a-single-parents-path-to-community/

3 Keys for Couples Navigating Life in an Empty Nest https://thetherapistgroup.com/2019/11/3-keys-for-couples-navigating-life-in-an-empty-nest/

The Mental Health Benefits of Journaling https://psychcentral.com/lib/the-health-benefits-of-journaling

Mindfulness exercises https://www.mayoclinic.org/healthy-lifestyle/consumer-health/in-depth/mindfulness-exercises/art-20046356

7 Best Mood Trackers to Chart and Journal Your ... https://positivepsychology.com/mood-charts-track-your-mood/

Five Science-Backed Strategies to Build Resiliencehttps://greatergood.berkeley.edu/article/item/five_science_backed_strategies_to_build_resilience

Kids Flown the Coop? 10 Not-So-Obvious Money Tips for ... https://www.pnc.com/insights/personal-finance/invest/money-tips-for-empty-nesters.html

Best Budgeting Apps Of October 2024 https://www.forbes.com/advisor/banking/best-budgeting-apps/

What Are the Pros and Cons of Using a 529 Plan? https://www.savingforcollege.com/article/what-are-the-pros-and-cons-of-using-a-529-plan

Downsizing for Retirement – 9 Downsizing Tips for Seniors https://www.actsretirement.org/resources-advice/finance-saving-money/downsizing-for-retirement/

Adults in Generation X who feel a sense of spiritual peace ... https://www.pewresearch.org/religious-landscape-study/database/frequency-of-feeling-spiritual-peace-and-wellbeing/at-least-once-a-week/generational-cohort/generation-x/

Millennials lead shift away from organized religion as ... https://www.cnbc.com/2021/12/29/millennials-lead-shift-away-from-organized-religion-as-pandemic-tests-faith.html

Meditation: A simple, fast way to reduce stress https://www.mayoclinic.org/tests-procedures/meditation/in-depth/meditation/art-20045858

The Impact of Gratitude on Mental Health https://namica.org/blog/the-impact-of-gratitude-on-mental-health/

Rising Housing Prices Force Adult Kids Back Home https://newsroom.thrivent.com/2024-04-30-Rising-Housing-Prices-Force-Adult-Kids-Back-Home-Thrivent-Study-Finds

Setting Win-Win Boundaries With Your Adult Child https://www.psychologytoday.com/ca/blog/liking-the-child-you-love/202307/setting-win-win-boundaries-with-your-adult-child

Better Together: Why multigenerational living is on the rise https://blog.atproperties.com/multigenerational-living-on-the-rise/

Your Adult Child at Home: Keeping the Dynamic Healthyhttps://www.forbes.com/sites/forbesbooksauthors/2024/03/28/your-adult-child-at-home-keeping-the-dynamic-healthy/

Maintaining Long-Distance Family Relationships as You Age https://www.canterburycourt.org/long-distance-families-senior-living/

Navigating the Changing Parent: Gen X vs. Millennial https://content.acsa.org/navigating-the-changing-parent-gen-x-vs-millennial/

Organizing a Successful Family Reunion https://jborganizing.com/organizing-tips/organizing-a-successful-family-reunion/

The Role of Grandparents in the Lives of Youth - PMC https://www.ncbi.nlm.nih.gov/pmc/articles/PMC3462462/

www.ingramcontent.com/pod-product-compliance
Ingram Content Group UK Ltd.
Pitfield, Milton Keynes, MK11 3LW, UK
UKHW022004190726
13853UKWH00004B/1731